Rethinking Monitoring and Evaluation

Challenges and Prospects in the
Changing Global Aid Environment

Rethinking Monitoring and Evaluation

Challenges and Prospects in the Changing Global Aid Environment

Esther Mebrahtu

Brian Pratt

Linda Lönnqvist

INTRAC
International NGO Training and Research Centre

INTRAC, the International NGO Training and Research Centre, was set up in 1991 to provide specially designed training, consultancy and research services to organisations involved in international development and relief. Our goal is to improve NGO performance by exploring policy issues and by strengthening management and organisational effectiveness.

First published in 2007 by

INTRAC
PO Box 563
Oxford
OX2 6RZ
United Kingdom

Tel: +44 (0)1865 201851
Fax: +44 (0)1865 201852
Email: info@intrac.org
Website: www.intrac.org

ISBN 9781905240104

Design and production by Jerry Burman 01803 845562

Cover design by Grounded Design

Illustrations by Linda Lönnqvist, www.developmentcartoons.com

Printed on demand 2020 by

Practical Action Publishing Ltd
27a Albert Street, Rugby, CV21 2SG, Warwickshire, UK
www.practicalactionpublishing.org

Preface and Acknowledgements

This book brings together the findings, debates, discussions and occasionally the disappointments which were all a part of the process of the *Sixth Conference on Evaluating Social Development* organised by INTRAC. At a time when so much of the focus of the aid industry is on a minimalist measur-ing of inputs and outputs, it seems that we still need to be reminded that t h e re is more to monitoring and evaluation than accounting for the resources used. The workshops and conference which preceded this book tried to capture some of the key debates at this time. Whether in the future this modest volume will be seen as the last attempt to ensure some serious consideration of the need to learn from the impact of development coop-eration, or alternatively a contribution towards re-valuing the roles of mon-itoring and evaluation, time will be the judge.

INTRAC wishes to thank all those who helped ensure the workshops were successful in bringing together participants from across Africa, Latin America, Europe and Asia: ActionAid Ghana, the Department of Social Sci-ences of the Pontificia Universidad Católica del Perú, the Swedish Interna-tional Development Cooperation Agency (Sida) and Part i c i p a t oryResearch in Asia (PRIA) in India.

Additionally we wish to thank those who contributed energy, ideas and resources to the final conference in the Netherlands. The full list of partic-ipants is in Appendix 2. However, specific thanks should go to the Catholic O rganisation for Relief and Development (Cordaid), Swedish Intern a t i o n a l Development Cooperation Agency (Sida), Norwegian Development Net-work, Concern Worldwide, MS Denmark, the Dutch Foreign Ministry, and the Canadian International Development Agency (CIDA) for their fin a n c i a l support.

In addition to the three of us who have tried to capture the findings and discussions we wish to acknowledge the considerable input from Oliver Bakewell who wrote the report on the European workshop, Lucy Earle who compiled the report on the Africa workshop, PRIA who provided the Asia workshop re p o rt, and Luis Soberon who captured the Lima workshop despite it being several times larger than we expected! Many of the rich and

detailed workshop and conference papers and presentations can be down-loaded free of charge from INTRAC's website at
www.intrac.org/pages/Past_Conferences.html.

Finally, thanks to Jerry Adams who helped throughout in both the planning and feeding in ideas, Zoë Wilkinson, the principal organiser and coordinator of the diverse events, and our other colleagues in INTRAC, many of whom played key roles in organisation, facilitation and support.

The Conference Process

Between the 3rd–5th of April 2006, 120 international delegates gathered in the Netherlands to attend INTRAC's *Sixth Evaluation Conference*. They rep-resented a broad cross-section of organisations and individuals involved in international development, including Civil Society Organisations (CSOs), i n t e rnational NGOs and their partners or affiliates, South-based NGOs, mis-sions, universities, official donor agencies and foundations.

The conference set out to assess and tackle the most prominent challenges to the operationalisation of monitoring and evaluation (M&E) faced by such organisations – which in many cases turned out to be the same old, stubbornly-unresolved challenges endured for the past few decades. The conference aspired to be a 'master-class' type event that dealt with a wide range of global M&E issues.

To this end, the theme (although not the structure) of the conference was kept deliberately open-ended, with more in-depth sessions scheduled for participants to flag upcoming issues in their specific realms of practice. The conference process was also deliberately open and iterative so that the programme content evolved in response to key outputs from earlier con-ference sessions.

One reason for this iterative process was to make the selected themes as relevant as possible for conference participants. The conference steering committee wanted to enable voices from different parts of the world to inform the emergent M&E discussions and to avoid an overly Northern or donor-centred perspective. In keeping with this intention the *Sixth Evaluation Conference* was preceded by four regional workshops held in four dif-ferent continents throughout 2005: in Ghana, India, Sweden and Peru. These focused on evolving M&E tensions and regional opportunities.

The African regional workshop, held at ActionAid in Accra, Ghana in April 2005, focused on issues to do with the M&E of advocacy programmes. The Latin American workshop in Lima, Peru in August of that year focused broadly on re-directing M&E principles towards the assessment of public programmes. This was hosted by the Catholic University of Lima. SIDA hosted the European workshop in Härnösand, Sweden (October 2005) where civil society organisations discussed the M&E issues that had had a significant impact on them in the past decade. Many of these issues appeared to relate to the identity crisis felt by Northern NGOs as they try to find their place within a rapidly changing aid environment. The Asian regional workshop was held in November 2005 at Participatory Research in Asia (PRIA) in New Delhi, India. This workshop explored the 'next genera-tion of M&E issues' and covered topics such as citizen monitoring, partic-ipatory impact assessment and the M&E of disaster and rehabilitation programmes.

A select number of key findings from the regional workshops were pre-sented in plenary sessions and at the 'marketplace', where participants exhibited their conclusions and had the opportunity to discuss these indi-vidually with browsing participants. The Regional Workshop feedback ses-sions were then used to flag issues that fuelled the ongoing discussions and analysis during the conference.

For many participants, the success of this conference lay not only its opportune timing (given the gathering pace of the harmonisation agenda of official aid agencies), but in its uniquely process- and interaction-focused approach. The first of its kind within the history of INTRAC conferences, the flexible and iterative methods we used at this event allowed partici-pants to create a hub or meeting-place for themselves with like-minded individuals, and consequently enriched the learning from their interac-tions. The dynamic methodologies (e.g. speed-networking, the market-place, café tables, gallery walls, cascade) employed throughout the three days were also popular and served to energise both co-ordinators and par-ticipants alike. The facilitators' notes for the conference methodologies are published in Appendix 1 for those who wish to make use of them at their own events.

We were fortunate to count on many inspiring and insightful contribu-tions to this event, all of which have helped shape the thinking behind this publication. In return, we hope that this book will stimulate thinking about

M&E beyond the current situation and highlight the vast array of opportunities that currently exist for strengthening this critical aspect of the
development process.

Brian Pratt, Esther Mebrahtu and Linda Lönnqvist
Oxford July 2007

Contents

Where we came from and how we got to this point

Brian Pratt and Linda Lönnqvist

For many years INTRAC has worked with a wide range of people from across the globe to explore the implications of innovations in the monitoring and evaluation of social development. We have done so because we have a shared belief in the importance of monitoring and evaluation (M&E) and because we see social development as a process of social change and transformation that lies at the heart of development. For us, development is not measured by economic indices of growth. Nor is it merely a question of physical infrastructure, better health or education or other improvements in peoples' lives, important though these are. For real, sustainable development to take place we need to look at long-term changes in the social constraints which hold groups of people in poverty and exclude them from the benefits of development. Because we see social development as more than just improved state health or education facilities, and more than just social welfare, we realised that new M&E systems would be required to assess, evaluate and learn from social development activities.

It was not an accident that impetus for social development and its M&E came primarily from NGOs, not state-based agencies. It was the activities of NGOs in the 1980s that challenged the accepted economist-dominated orthodoxy which simplistically tied development to infrastructural investments to encourage investment and trade. The recent re-emergence of this view of development[1] is a reason why we have found ourselves defending client-based approaches to M&E. We have also argued for basing development concepts on social change, which in our approach to M&E has always been one of our definitions of 'impact'.[2]

Background to Previous INTRAC Conferences on M&E

The conviction that evaluation is a key aspects of the process of development has always been one of the driving forces behind our interest in trying to show that evaluation is not a necessary evil, but in itself a positive contribution to development. Years ago Brian Pratt wrote a paper entitled *The Evaluation of Social Development or Evaluation as Social Development*[3] which he argued that properly implemented evaluation could and should be a major part of effective social development. This idea led us to concepts like empowerment and to discussions around the role of evaluator as facilitator. We entered the debate about the degree to which social 'facts' are fixed immutably, or whether they are open to socially determined interpretation. We realised we had entered dangerous ground fought over by philosophers and scientists about the positivistic (absolute) nature of knowledge, compared to a more interpretative or relativist approach. In other words we looked for the right ground in the spectrum between those expecting evaluation to produce objective hard facts – and those who hold back and argue that nothing is ever totally objective and that facts are malleable.

Each of the six conferences we have had on the subject has been a child of its times. Development paradigms and politics influence M&E and it is interesting to chart how conferences have reflected contemporary thinking while providing nodes of thought that inspire participants to influence contemporary trends.

Aid policy fluctuations and civil society M&E

Aid policy fluctuations are the bane of continuity in development work. While everyone in the sector recognises that change takes an age to set in

1. Easterly W. (2006) provides a good review of this backwards trend in economic thinking.
2. Bakewell O. et al. (2003) pp.19–20 summarise our views on this.
3. Pratt. B. (1989) unpublished University of Swansea lecture.

motion, and that slow and steady is the only way to make changes 'stick', new self-professed paradigm shifts in development policy come along at regular intervals. Each change in thinking means a major reorientation as development policies, themes and M&E practice percolate downwards from major development institutions to aid recipient countries and NGOs.

Technocratic and grassroots values struggle for control of the future of M&E.

Some of these shifts are about themes – from democratisation to debt relief to trade justice, for example. There are also 'waves' of new initiatives such as NEPAD (the New Economic Partnership for Africa's Development)[4], the Millennium Declaration and the Millennium Development Goals (MDGs), the Paris Declaration and Paris Agenda on Aid Effectiveness[5] as well as 'presidential projects' associated with individual politicians – such as the Commission for Africa or the Africa Growth and Opportunity Act (AGOA).[6]

---

4. An Africa-initiated economic development and governance framework that was established in 2001.

5. The Paris Declaration in 2005 set in motion the aid effectiveness agenda, aiming to make the distribution of bilateral aid more cost-effective and focused on beneficiary governments' priorities. Its five basic principles are ownership; managing for results; mutual accountability; alignment and harmonisation.

6. AGOA, enacted by the USA in 2000, gives African countries access to US markets in return for implementing free market policies.
www.agoa.gov

Other deeper changes are about approaches and the importance of such concepts as empowerment, ownership, accountability, good governance, well-being or national security as foundations of successful development. Wider shifts also include efforts to mainstream 'cross-cutting' issues such as gender and the environment and incorporate them into all aspects of development practice. With changes happening constantly along all these different axes, all development actors are feeling the push and pull of new initiatives. Each stream of thinking seizes on one of the myriad aspects of real life and singles it out as the key to improvements. This has a noticeable impact on how civil society organisations (CSOs) undertake M&E. The logical framework matrix came in with the trend for results-based management. In contrast, participatory monitoring follows more grassroots-focused 'ownership' thinking.

Changes in management debates outside the development sector have also left their mark on M&E. There has been a shift in management thinking from rational management by objectives – e.g. logframes and results-based management – to power-conscious management that acknowledges that reality is messy and uncertain, and considers the many different perspectives involved. This broader type of management does not simply focus on systems and processes, but takes into account values, loyalties and history. Such thinking has influenced the use of stakeholder and network analysis, helped identify drivers of change and tipping points, facilitated scaling-up from projects to programmes and policy and has incorporated learning and mainstreaming into the project cycle.[7] However, this approach seems to be in decline. It is telling that 'managing for results', a classic example of rational management, has now become a central principle for aid management and is one of the five principles of the topical Paris Declaration.

As macro-policies have changed, so too have views on the importance of civil society. CSOs, especially development NGOs, are generally considered to be 'close to the people' and the perceived 'value-added' they bring to development often stems from this image of flexibility, listening, social development and accountability to beneficiaries. The position, influence and room for manoeuvre of civil society depends on current development paradigms – the *zeitgeist* – and the political composition of major donors

---

7. Personal communication from Dr James Copestake, Senior Lecturer, University of Bath

and CSOs' efforts to influence agendas. CSOs tend to be associated with 'soft' values and their fortunes wax and wane with the prominence of 'soft' thinking in wider development policy. In contrast, NGOs are not associated with large-scale, national-level initiatives or national economy – the domain of the state – or private sector development, i.e. markets.

NGO influence hinges on political relationships between large providers of official development assistance (ODA) and recipient countries and whether or not civil society can be used to keep governments in check – or vice versa. Some development actors see civil society as the champion of grassroots democracy, a counterweight to the corruption-riddled state, while the other end of the spectrum considers CSOs to be illegitimate troublemakers and urges them to eschew politics and focus on providing maternal health advice, support for the deaf, or other similar services.

Civil society thrives when ideals of participation, grassroots engagement, long-term impact and empowerment are in the ascendance, but less so when rational management approaches – stressing results, large-scale delivery, macroeconomics and multilateral aid policy – are in vogue. When contemporary development thinking follows 'soft' values donors give CSOs more autonomy. Civil society is on a short leash, however, when orthodoxy stresses the economic and the provision of measurable short-term outputs.

There are thus three areas where changes impact on M&E: the way international development cooperation is *structured,* the way in which it is *regarded* and changes in M&E as a *field of practice.*

This shows the importance of policy context. It was evident from the latest evaluation conference INTRAC convened that the most pressing issues now are decentralisation and partnership, aid effectiveness, security thinking, the pressure of accountability much 'further upwards' towards donor country taxpayers, and the increasing complexity and professionalisation of NGO work. These will be dealt with in more detail in the section on the sixth conference below.

INTRAC's M&E Conferences – mirroring and influencing development trends

As our successive evaluation conferences have demonstrated, M&E reflects the development discourse that it seeks to understand, codify, analyse and interpret. This may seem obvious in many ways, but many people feel that their own small area of knowledge is independent of other debates when in reality they are often affected by debates they may be completely unaware of. It is therefore important that we look at M&E within the context of other development discourses.

We will throughout this book refer back to the sixth conference, where we realised that the discourse on M&E seemed to have fragmented. We will explore some of the reasons why we think this has happened and also analyse some of the ways this has manifested itself. The apparent absence of clear consensus over the roles, techniques of M&E is a challenge to us all. It has led the sponsors of the conference and the present editorial group[8] to reflect on what has happened since the 1980s when we held the first conference on evaluating social development and how debates in development affected our meetings.

The conferences are not the proceedings of a professional association where people attend to sell their wares and services, to indulge in professional reinforcement and intellectual back slapping. Had we gone down this road we would have closed ranks against outsiders, created constraints on people joining our group, imposed professional, ostensibly well-thought through but ultimately arbitrary rules governing membership and agreed to market a shared vision of M&E.

This was never going to be our style. We sought people from across the globe involved in M&E. Some were professional evaluators whose incomes came from regularly engaging in evaluations. Others managed evaluations, some had had one-off evaluation experience while others were resentful or grateful victims/recipients of evaluations. Each time we met, the group was different except for a small core of participants who attended several conferences. The nature of the group illustrated differences in who was engaging in M&E, what their concerns were and what they felt they had to share. In understanding the sixth conference we felt it valuable to look back and reflect on procedures and outcomes of earlier meetings.

---

8. In addition to the authors, this group included Oliver Bakewell, Jerry Adams and Anne Garbutt.

The First M&E Conference – 'How to evaluate'

The first conference held in 1989 came at a time when many of us were challenging what we saw as the dominance of development discussions by the large official agencies. Nearly all the debates were managed by the large multi- and bilateral agencies. If others were in attendance it was by invitation. It was hard forever being an outsider, on the margins of official events, struggling to find a voice and ways to illustrate alternative thinking and practice. Our initial conference – never regarded at the time as the first of a series – was clearly seen as an attempt by NGOs and academics to hold a meeting independent of the big players. The sponsors were a group of European NGOs and independent consultants and academics. That it was held in a university, Swansea, was almost an accident, and was a decision made because one of us had a job there and the university could offer logistical support. We were able to provide space to a range of speakers from different organisation, large and small, from across the globe.

The issues we tackled were, in many ways, basic. We talked about the role of the 'evaluator', what made a good evaluator and why they were often seen so negatively. We looked at issues of process and planning and the specific challenges of development evaluation. At a more profound level we realised that in the 'mainstream agencies' M&E was treated as a very technical exercise. It was still at the level of quantifying products – crop yields, water flow, and vaccine rates – with limited thinking about social development – gender differentials, community cohesion and empowerment. We also realised that once we looked to social development issues we found that the old positivistic approach to development and its M&E looked very inadequate. We thus developed a more interpretative approach to evaluation which entailed engaging clients/beneficiaries – who later came to be known as 'stakeholders' – in processes of social development and its evaluation.[9]

Second Conference – 'There is an alternative!'

The second conference was organised almost as a direct follow-up to the first with a single simple aim – to provide examples of the practical methods,

---

9. The conference was summarised in Marsden, D. and Oakley, P. (1990)

techniques and approaches people had found useful in implementing a more participatory, people-based form of evaluation. The title of the conference publication, 'Measuring the Process'[10] says it all. We realised that there was no single method for evaluation, but a rich array of approaches used by groups in different contexts. The best we could do was illustrate some approaches through case studies so people could choose which might be relevant to their needs.

The first conference was an initial statement that it was both possible and necessary to develop an independent forum for discussion and an alternative to the traditional development M&E mainstream. The second conference was a clear attempt to satisfy practitioners that there was a range of methods they could use and that our previous conference was based on experience and not just theory. The second conference in 1992 came at a time when NGOs had gone through massive growth. Suddenly they were no longer the poor cousins following in the wake of the official agencies. There was an increased demand for alternative M&E to match the growth of alternative development programming. The mainstream couldn't cope with the needs of agencies. Narrow quantitative methods seemed inadequate at a time when paradigms and approaches to development were being challenged. There was a great deal of deconstructing of previous development thinking. It was no longer sufficient to measure crop yields and income levels. People wanted to know who benefited from these presumed gains and how incomes were distributed within households and communities. To gain answers to these and a multitude of other questions required new techniques which would allow us to disaggregate our responses by gender, age, ethnicity, caste, class or other variable. Gross figures were no longer sufficient.

A great deal of what we then discussed focussed on the emerging use of participatory M&E techniques. These had not been hitherto unknown, but the advent of PRA (Participatory Rural Appraisal) led to a new energy around participation.

10. Marsden, D., Oakley P. and Pratt, B. (1994)

The Third conference: M&E – 'So What?'

'The current debates that surround evaluation of development projects are embedded in wider debates about authority, legitimacy, transparency and accountability'.

(Marsden, Oakley and Pratt 1994)

This statement formed both the conclusion to the second conference and the opening statement for the book based on the third! The repetition of this key principle was intended to ensure that practitioners understood that whatever methods they adhered to or 'tools' they used, these could not be divorced or disassociated from the context in which the evaluation and the programme being evaluated were constituted. In the process around the third conference we could see already widening gaps between approaches. Although many concepts of social development participatory M&E were being accepted by an increasing range of agencies there was opposition. It was still being argued that the two forms of accountability were getting in each other's way. Attempts to encourage accountability to clients were regarded by some as reducing accountability to donors and treasuries and vice versa. People seemed to agree that both were compatible but the reality seemed somewhat different. Indeed we were already seeing a divide between rhetoric of participation and the reality of a tendency of agencies to pull back to constant, established rules and forms and procedures. We questioned whether this was because of a general failure of development organisations across the board to really engage with and implement M&E systems. A plethora of studies seem to indicate that NGOs and others were not actually improving their M&E systems at all, and as such were in danger of both poor accountability *and* poor learning from their experience. (Tendler 1982, Riddell 1997, Smillie 1995, Surr 1995).

What the third conference set out to do was to look beyond the M&E of activities (outputs) towards outcomes and impact. In other words, were there experiences in M&E which could enlighten and encourage us all to look positively and realistically and assess whether we were really helping to make changes in poverty, social exclusion and gender inequalities. We found ourselves revisiting what we meant by social development and in doing so attempted to rescue the term from those who used it simply to refer to social welfare and social service provision.

We wanted to bring the transformative and empowering element back into social development. This also had implications for the evaluation of outcomes and impacts in that it set sights much higher. It asked us not only to look at whether we had really delivered a service to poor people but posed another key question: 'Have we actually done anything to mitigate the previous poverty conditions?' The key word became change: had we helped change the lives of marginalised people in a long-lasting manner and, if so, could we monitor, measure and understand these changes? We posed in simple terms the 'so what' question. Did all our activity (well-managed or not) actually make a difference to the lives of poor people?

Fortunately there were sufficient people genuinely concerned with answering the *'So what'* question for us to provide some ideas on how to move forwards with evaluating outcomes and impacts. Several of the larger INGO groups had been working on methodologies for impact assessment. In retrospect, it is perhaps significant that the major attempts to engage with impact evaluation described in the book were by NGOs despite an exhaustive review of official agency approaches to M&E by Peter Oakley in preparation for the conference.[11]

It would be an exaggeration to claim that these debates on impact led to a major change in the practice of a large number of agencies. However, many did commit resources to establishing lessons learned and assessing whether different types of programme had had positive outcomes or tackled the problems they had set out to mitigate. If we were constrained at all in taking forward ideas around impact it was because there was still a tension between accountability and learning. Given the methodological difficulties of assessing impact, and associated costs entailed in impact evaluation, common sense would indicate that rather than trying to introduce impact evaluation as a standard procedure, we should sample programme and other development experiences and collate our findings into meta-evaluations. This apparently sensible solution to a resource constraint does not satisfy those who insist on standardised accountability package for all interventions. Thus the desire for basic accountability often gets in the way of desires to reduce the number of evaluations in favour of more in-depth reviews of impact.

A second issue which came out of the review of impact evaluations is a

---

11. Oakley, P. Pratt. B. and Clayton, A. (1998)

problem constantly discussed in international development and also, one suspects, in public sector management – impatience to know what has happened almost before a programme or policy has been introduced. The time span of development cooperation has always been constrained by project cycles sometimes lasting less than a year – especially problematic given the enthusiastic embrace of embracing of quick impact programmes (QIPs). By the time programmes come to an end, policies, fads, jargon and ideas have moved on. In the haste to adopt the new, the old is ignored. Learning, instead of being added to and compounded, is relegated to historical archives.

Fourth Conference – evaluating empowerment

Throughout the first three conferences we always tried to maintain the idea of social development as transformation. In the fourth conference we went further by looking critically at the concept of empowerment and how to evaluate it. This was a voyage of discovery which took us across several continents. We held workshops in Peru, Bangladesh, Tanzania, Sri Lanka, Jordan, Nicaragua, Indonesia and Sweden where we explored the concept of evaluating empowerment. We realised that empowerment has to be context-relevant and to that end we used case studies from Nicaragua, Tanzania, Egypt, and Bangladesh and explored them in the different workshops.[12]

This methodology enabled us to explore both the method for evaluating empowerment in each context and to choose locally appropriate indicators. We were able to avoid the common confusion between indicators and the methods used to collect them. The workshops showed that by agreeing common definitions and adopting a shared approach to evaluating empowerment even something as potentially difficult and intangible could be understood and evaluated. We remained aware that specific indicators used would have to be derived from the individual culture and context.

In the concluding section of the book which summarises the debates from the conference and workshop,[13] Peter Oakley makes the interesting point that 'empowerment' is often used in different ways, including

---

12. Oakley, P. and Clayton, A. (2000) includes the case studies and workshop methodology.
13. Oakley, P. (ed.), (2001)

empowerment as, participation, capacity building, economic improvement, individual empowerment and as democratisation. What strikes one in retrospect is that we were still assuming development to be about people and that sets of relationships, social and cultural goals were key to development. Participants realised that 'power' was at the heart of development and its evaluation. This did not always sit comfortably with existing M&E systems which were geared towards measuring improvements in terms of the physical environment, services and production. We concluded that:

> 'Empowerment is to do with change and few development agencies are currently able to "measure" social change as a result of project interventions. ... it is recognised that the only people who can authentically assess change in power relations are those whose livelihoods are directly affected. However, current M&E systems simply do not allow for such a shift in focus ...'[14]

The nub of the problem seemed to be because agencies were unable to evaluate empowerment, and did not want to engage in activities they could not measure, they shied away from empowerment initiatives. The idea that responsibility for evaluating impact and empowerment could be passed to those affected was for many agencies a step too far.

In reviewing the whole exercise in the eight workshops and the fourth international conference, we realised that there are many practitioners who understand that issues of power are a critical dimension of poverty, but that few development agencies have placed empowerment at the heart of their programmes. Agencies and development personnel avoid the issue by assuming that what they do will contribute to empowerment, whether through capacity building or service delivery programmes. Evidence suggests, however, that unless empowerment is a conscious, rather than implied, objective it is unlikely to be achieved. We concluded that without a far more assertive and conscious process to engage with power issues the entire development community would continue to fail to address the key issues of power inequalities.

It seems an increasing number of current development interventions are power-blind, for they assume that technical interventions will lead to social change. Is this because agencies are intimidated by the challenges of con-

---

14. Ibid. p179.

fronting power inequalities? Could it be a political decision to desist from such a challenge or merely the inertia of large organisations unable to cope with any challenges at all? Another factor is that in the post-Cold War period – with Marxist analysis no longer in vogue – people and institutions do not feel that they have an alternative analytical framework with which to deal with power imbalances.

The Fifth International Conference 2003

The general problems faced by organisations regarding M&E became the focus of the fifth conference. Debates were characterised as a tension between 'participative evaluation' and 'managerial performance systems'. One of the main challenges for the conference was whether we could reconcile the need for client-based[15] learning and accountability with requirements for upwards accountability to donors and treasuries, or even if these two different approaches could be reconciled at all. We explored whether the predominance of top-down performance assessment measurement systems which were tied to bureaucratic demands for accountability and efficiency undermined a desire for maximum impact for clients or primary stakeholders.

Although we sought to encapsulate views from these two polarised options, we found from the outset that conference debates and discussions kept bringing us back to an interest in the first-hand experiences of participatory forms of M&E. In the conference book edited by Lucy Earle[16] it is clear to see where the energy lay – the way participants shared experiences and their stories of what had worked and what had not. Thus the conference became a learning experience in itself.

> We faced difficulties in trying to analyse why people found it difficult, if not impossible, to reconcile the competing experiences of performance assessment and accountability to funders, against participation with clients/beneficiaries. We noted general agreement that accountability is sacrosanct. All agencies, whether NGOs or government departments, must account for the scarce resources at their disposal. To be accountable financially is not some-

---

15. We tend to use the term 'client-based', rather than the more passive terms 'beneficiary' or 'poor'.
16. Earle, L. (ed.) 2004).

thing very complex; we merely need to prove that we spent the funds we received for the purposes for which they were approved. Thereupon it is a matter of collating and verifying receipts and cross checking activities carried out against plans ... .[17]

It would appear that much of accountability for performance assessment has adopted the partial and artificial measure of financial accountability.

We recognised that many organisations, whether private, public or voluntary, talk about organisational learning but only pay lip service to learning from mistakes. There seems consensus that we need to be both accountable and to learn from our work and that M&E can help us do so. However, both accountability and learning tended to be seen as 'upwards' to the source of funds, whether to an external donor or internal government treasury. The key lesson from debates around participation and subsequently empowerment and citizen rights is the importance of both accountability and learning. Earlier conferences captured some of these ideas both conceptually and practically through case studies and other experiences. The value of client participation in M&E has been increasingly recognised.

'So where is the problem?', Brian Pratt asks in the afterword to the conference book. In essence, he said:

'it lies in the structure of an industry which is inherently competitive at the level of the sponsors but unfortunately, not at the level of clients.'[18]

Marginalised people seldom have much say in what they receive, who they would prefer to deliver it and what they think of the quality and effectiveness of the services provided.

'In contrast, private businesses are generally obliged to compete for clients, putting a certain degree of power into the clients' hands.'[19]

As we examined the tension between managerial performance assessments and client-based systems during the fifth conference we found that this was not the key issue. The problem lay not so much in the ability of develop-

---

17. Earle L. (ed.) (2004), Afterword by Brian Pratt p.155.
18. Ibid p.156
19. Ibid p.156

ment agencies to support participation but, rather, their inability to escape from the constraints of unwieldy M&E systems which failed to tell them whether they were really having intended impacts on the lives of poor people.

As a sector we continue to work with procedures and approaches poorly adapted from dated military and private sector practice. Why do we do so when they have not been found to be useful? The answer derives from the reality that most development agencies are in competition for funds. They are thus primarily concerned to meet the requirements of donors and to demonstrate accountability to them, rather than focusing on investment in strong M&E systems based on honesty and participation. What surprised many was that this is not just a phenomenon of small struggling community groups, but seems to characterise much larger public sector agencies and international NGOs. The fifth conference unleashed much energy and shared experience, but few attendees wanted to dwell on the cumbersome, hard-to-defend procedures and systems which actually dominate their working lives. Dr Pratt concludes:

> 'So, whilst donors increasingly demand the use of standard approaches to accountability and learning, based on systems no one has been able to make work successfully, even after 25 years of trying, we have an aid industry moving towards funding mechanisms that will make it even easier for the corrupt to ignore clients, accountability and learning ... . Meanwhile, CS groups find that their innovation and energy is sapped by inappropriate monitoring systems that reveal very little about what actually happens in their groups and programmes'.[20]

At the end of the fifth conference we felt that we needed to encourage some new thinking. It was agreed we needed a reality check and to explore through a series of regional workshops what aspects of M&E were of concern in different parts of the world. Therefore we proposed a departure from previous practice by agreeing a new structure for the sixth evaluation conference: instead of agreeing in advance a set theme we decided to use exploratory methods to shape an iterative process whereby workshop participants identified the key issues to be discussed.

---

20. Ibid. p.158.

Sixth Evaluation Conference 2006

In retrospect we can see that what we didn't allow for was the widening gap between those directly engaged in development in developing and transitional countries and those burdened by the responsibilities of accountability to resource providers. The workshops around the world – which are described in the chapters that follow[21] – produced a rich array of issues for discussion and analysis. We were overwhelmed by the response to the regional workshops. The multiple themes identified ranged from the M&E of advocacy, through to humanitarian work, even the role of the media, as well as experiments in citizen-level monitoring. We realised that while issues varied from country to country we had many concerns in common.

One issue about which, unusually perhaps, there was little discussion was the commonly perceived 'tyranny of donors' which so often is blamed for most issues and constraints regarding M&E. However, this did come to the fore in Sweden when international NGOs (INGOs) met with official agencies. Both groups seemed to feel the other was the obstacle to making progress in devising more user-friendly M&E systems. Role confusion was also apparent as participants seemed unsure whether they were development workers, activists or donors.

This lack of clarity unsurprisingly coloured discussions as to the role of INGOs in the M&E process. The role of an agency in M&E will vary depending on its role in the overall development process. This may be self-evident but it is often not realised. In part this is due to a widespread genuine confusion but also to a tension between the roles people want to play, as opposed to those they are institutionally obliged to play. These tensions made it difficult for international agencies representatives, constrained by accountability requirements and distant from direct relationships with clients. To make matters worse, they are in competition with each other, and not just within their own sectors. The UN competes with INGOs and they both compete for bilateral and multilateral funds. The safe option in the face of such competition is to play safe!

These tensions and growing divide between some of the key development actors are apparent in the field of M&E. Thus we have a reversion to strict, often quantitative, monitoring systems which are limited to

---

21. Ghana, Peru, India, Sweden.

measuring activities delivered against plans. These are understandable requirements of the sub-contract culture but often lead to all energy being focused on showing compliance with deliverables, with very little effort left for reviewing outcomes or impact. The incentive structure is around meeting short-term targets and within M&E to identifying 'tools to do this'.

However, there are still some, perhaps many, development workers trying to get to grips with the 'so what question' in terms of determining the impact of so many years of hard work. Practitioners are realising that answering, or even attempting to answer, the 'so what' questions, will need a range of approaches which engage with clients, that go well beyond monitoring the achievement of delivery targets. In terms of M&E, the debates are around sharing experiences of how people managed this process. Participants were thus as interested in the processes we ourselves used in the sixth conference as in the content itself.

Sixth conference and beyond – policy issues impacting M&E today

To take the discussions from the sixth evaluation conference forward requires examination of civil society's engagement in aid policy processes and the impact of key policy trends: aid effectiveness and security.

Civil society engagement with aid debates

While Northern NGOs have become increasingly engaged with issues regarding aid architecture and proposals for reform, Southern CSO engagement has been patchy at best. In its 2005 report *Real Aid: An Agenda for Making Aid Work* ActionAid called for the creation of a new International Aid Agreement:

> 'that replaces the prevailing top-down, donor-dominated model with a system of genuine mutual accountability that balances the legitimate interests of donors, recipients and, most importantly, poor people'.

Other networks, most notably Reality of Aid,[22] have attempted to build a dialogue between CSOs in the North and the South and lobby for policies and practices in the international aid regime that benefit the poor.

For the most part, however, the voices of aid recipients in shaping such trends have been muted. Their contribution to debate on how to reform the aid system has been rather limited. This is in marked contrast to the substantial involvement and significant contribution Southern CSOs have made to debates and discussion surrounding debt cancellation (see Lifuka 2005, for example).

This is despite the emergence of the word 'participation' in high-level aid instruments such as Poverty Reduction Strategy Papers (PRSPs) and the Paris Declaration. Southern CSOs seem to be particularly sensitive on this issue, feeling that civil society voices and input are often marginalised in national-level development negotiations. Zie Gariyo of the Uganda Debt Network illustrates this in an analysis he wrote on Uganda's PRSP experience. He contends that 'most civil society organisations and institutions lack capacity to engage donors and policy planners in meaningful dialogue about policy issues. Both at national and local levels this is still a problem. The danger therefore is that CSOs might end up endorsing positions for which they have little knowledge' (Gariyo 2002). There are civil society efforts underway to avoid duplicating the PRS processes' lack of real consultation in the emerging aid effectiveness agenda. CSOs, including African organisations and networks, are mobilising to lobby the Paris Agenda process and are planning parallel civil society events. Nonetheless, the real options for civil society influence over aid effectiveness decisions are thin on the ground.[23]

One explanation for the lack of Southern inputs in policy-level aid dialogue may be the lack of incentives to participate and the reality that transaction costs are significant, but potential payoffs uncertain. Conference participants expressed profound scepticism that anything they could propose would in fact shape, other than marginally, the actions of rich countries and the international organisations they dominate.

At the sixth conference discussions about the first theme – external

---

22. The global aid analysis network
www.realityofaid.org
23. See e.g. INTRAC (2007).

issues – highlighted the crucial importance of such engagement. If voices from the South are not heard, their omission from the debate is a missed opportunity to reform the international aid system and make it more responsive to the needs of the poor.

Where formal national accountability institutions are weak civil society often feels incapable and denied opportunities to either influence or track public finance decisions. Civil society is, thus, often excluded from a process which is largely carried out in private, bureaucrat-to-bureaucrat meetings of unaccountable civil servants.

Aid effectiveness

Among both donors and recipient country governments, a growing consensus has emerged on what needs to be done to make assistance work better. At the High-Level Forum on Aid Effectiveness held in Paris in March 2005, donor and recipient countries renewed pledges made in the Rome Declaration on Harmonisation of 2003 to improve levels of coordination and to minimise the negative effects of fragmented and unpredictable aid flows. The resulting *Paris Declaration on Aid Effectiveness* was signed by 61 bilateral and multilateral donors, 56 aid recipient countries and 14 CSOs – although some of these have distanced themselves from the Declaration and pointed out that their presence at the Paris High Level Forum is not the same as their endorsement. The Development Assistance Committee of the Organisation for Economic Cooperation and Development (OECD-DAC) has developed indicators to measure progress on aid effectiveness and promote greater mutual accountability (OECD-DAC 2005).

The Paris Declaration is seen by many observers as representing significant progress in establishing 'a set of monitorable targets for changes in donor, recipient, and joint behaviour' which could well embody 'the core of a new compact on mutual accountability' (Rogerson 2005a). In particular, signatories made a commitment to five principles to reform delivery of development assistance:

i)   recipient-country *ownership* of the development agenda

ii) a stress on *mutual accountability* between donor and recipient countries

iii) an ethos of *managing for results*

iv) donor *alignment* with the priorities and goals set by partner countries and increased reliance on national administration systems (aid *alignment)*

v) more co-ordinated, streamlined and harmonised actions among multiple donors (aid *harmonisation).*

It is becoming ever more apparent that recipient governments and their respective CSOs need to be proactive as efforts are made to put into practice the kind of laudable objectives set out in the Paris Declaration. The increasingly popular methodology of civil society monitoring was brought up time and again by conference participants who see it as an excellent opportunity for CSOs to contribute to the evolving structure. The key role of northern NGOs in putting pressure on their governments to be more transparent and accountable was also frequently highlighted, as was the need to ensure that public administration approaches do not undermine accountability.

Aid effectiveness requires strong country ownership. Extensions to this approach in the context of the *Paris Declaration on Aid Effectiveness* oblige donors to base their aid programmes on country-owned strategies. Under the rubric of 'alignment', donors also commit to greater use of national management systems. It is vital to ask whether 'national ownership' simply means control by the current government or the whole country – to what extent civil society and other actors can participate.

External actors are also asked in the Paris Declaration to coordinate their approaches to aid delivery and to commit to longer-term, reliable aid disbursement. Macro-level, government-centred aid mechanisms, notably direct budget support and sector-based programmatic approaches,[24] are best suited to Paris Declaration thinking.

However, from the perspective of aid recipients it is not immediately obvious that grouping donors together under a common umbrella, pursuing the same set of conditions, is always in a country's best interests. The risks of facing a united panel of donors – or a donor 'cartel' – could

---

24. Budget support is where aid money is paid directly to the Ministry of Finance to be spent as the country sees fit. Sector-wide approaches, or SWAps, are systems where donors who are funding, for example, education pay aid money directly to the Ministry of Education budget, and coordinate which areas will be funded – such multi-donor funding is called 'basket funding'.

potentially outweigh savings made by not having to deal with multiple aid sources separately. Likewise, a donor consensus is likely to follow the priorities of the donor in the strongest bargaining position, and many smaller country donors are wary of harmonising fundamental aspects of their ODA, preferring to keep their coordination at the procedures level.[25]

Potential Opportunities and Consequences of the Paris Agenda: What Role for Monitoring and Evaluation?

Participants at the sixth conference questioned the link between the Paris agenda and the MDGs it is intended to support. There were no satisfactory answers. They asked critical questions about the indicators against which this support could be measured and who has responsibility for such an assessment process. Sessions on Theme 1 of the conference (The Wider Context Affecting M&E) ended by concluding that there never been a more critical time for M&E to 'stand-up and be counted'. Never before has M&E had the opportunity to play such a critical role and to help ensure that:

i) we do not ignore essential lessons of the past (e.g. awareness of the significant limitations of mechanistic approaches to M&E and technocratic indicators)

ii) such technocratic methods do not overwhelm client-based participatory techniques

iii) we continue to learn from our mistakes by transparent self-critical analysis.

Region-specific discussions throughout the conference revealed the shared view that donors need to become more transparent when they allocate funds, and more accountable for their performance and the pledges they make. As stated in the *NGO Statement on Aid Effectiveness* (2005), which was signed by 26 Northern and Southern NGOs prior to the High-Level Forum in Paris, 'donors and recipients share responsibility for making aid work'. The aid system needs to be transformed from one that is based on one-sided conditionality to one built around mutual accountability. This emphasis

---

25. Personal communication from Finnish Ministry of Foreign Affairs, March 2007

on mutual accountability is essential if we are to shift – in the phrase coined by Rueben Lifuka of Africa Dialogue in Zambia – from donor-recipient relations based on tutelage to a genuine partnership among equals (Lifuka 2005).

> 'All donor conditions must be made public so that vital parliamentary and civil society oversight and input can be ensured'
>
> (NGO Paris Statement, in Lifuka 2005).

The key issue, then, is what kinds of mechanisms can be instituted to promote recipient governments' and CSOs' ability to monitor donor behaviour.

The dwindling flows of project finance may have serious negative repercussions on NGOs who had previously depended on such 'venture capital' to fund their own operations. However, the shift towards budget support could also give too much power to recipient governments in selecting priority projects and subcontractors, ending the direct relationship NGOs and donors have hitherto had with communities. Northern policymakers assume that new, more flexible aid instruments have, in principle, some degree of support. In practice, however, many Southern CSO actors have misgivings.

National Security Discourse in Development

Parallel with the changing methods of channelling aid funds to the South, is another emerging trend in international development: geopolitical security.[26] In the discourse of many donors today, 'conflict resolution', 'security' and even 'poverty eradication' are increasingly intermingled with notions of 'terrorism' and 'defence'. In the words of a controversial OECD-DAC paper in early 2002,

> 'development cooperation has an important role to play in helping to deprive terrorists of popular support and addressing the conditions that terrorist leaders feed on and exploit.'

It seems that the commitment made by world leaders gathered at the Mil-

---

26. This discourse is especially ambiguous since it uses the same term as 'human security', an entirely different, human-centred approach to development.

lennium Summit to 'spare no effort' for poverty eradication – an impetus supported by international human rights and humanitarian law – has been virtually cast aside. The case for increasing aid to alleviate policy has been hijacked by the demand for ever greater human, financial and military resources to guard against the threat of terrorist attacks on Northern states. Some donor countries, following the new mantra 'you can't have development without security', have concluded that security concerns must be prioritised and incorporated in all aspects of foreign policy, including development cooperation. This is most evident in OECD data showing aid allocations by country in recent years: humanitarian assistance and reconstruction following the wars in Afghanistan and Iraq have captured more than a third of the new aid resources allocated by donors since 2001.[27] As a result of this conflation of development, global security and anti-terrorism, the integrity of development assistance for poverty eradication is at risk.

Even more disconcerting, however, is the shrinking policy space available to citizen activism in repressive countries, since the 'war on terror' provides a potent weapon for unscrupulous governments to brand protesters as 'terrorist' and clamp down on their activities.[28]

The key issues explored by the 2006 *Reality of Aid Report* regarding the convergence of the peace, security and development agenda leads us to question: What is a rights-based approach to the nexus between human development and security? Whose security are we really protecting, in whose interests and at the expense of what? Is development cooperation repeating its Cold War history, and once again becoming a crude extension of donor foreign and defence policy? To what extent is donor aid increasingly implemented as 'risk management' for national security? It is increasingly apparent that the 'war on terror' has been used to justify practices that undermine the achievement of development goals. However, the real impact on aid allocations and the nature of donor cooperation with developing countries is only beginning to become apparent.

As we digest the information from the sixth conference, we have learned that as aid thinking influences aid delivery, hitherto accepted M&E

---

27. Figures compiled from the OECD aid database,
www.oecd.org/dataoecd/50/17/5037721.htm
and The Reality of Aid report (2006), pp. 235–239.
28. See e.g. Ontrac 35 and INTRAC briefing papers from autumn 2007.
www.intrac.org/docs/Ontrac_35.pdf

methods are being declared to be obsolete. Participation and long-term impact are falling out of favour; the logical framework matrix is in ascendance again. As Europeans elect increasingly conservative governments, the pressure is on to demonstrate tangible short term results in order to justify increases of aid towards 0.7% of GDP. It is highly unfortunate that this is at the expense of efforts to engage with social development through transforming social inequalities, injustice and involves abandonment of the quest to ensure long-term impacts from aid programmes.

2

Africa and the M&E of Power Relations

Linda Lönnqvist and Esther Mebrahtu

This chapter on monitoring advocacy and power relations in African civil society draws on findings from a monitoring and evaluation (M&E) workshop co-convened by INTRAC and ActionAid in Ghana in 2005, and the Africa group discussion at the sixth evaluation conference in the Netherlands. It looks at:

- power relations and accountability
- facilitator and donor manipulation
- ownership and use of tools
- the importance of critical thinking
- documentation, writing and oral M&E
- informal observation and the 'M&E mystique'.

The chapter starts with an overview of development aid in Africa, specifically covering the roles of international NGOs (INGOs), African NGOs and NGO advocacy. This background leads in to an in-depth discussion of CSOs' experiences of M&E on the ground.

Aid to Africa

Africa is widely considered to be the most disadvantaged, underdeveloped and aid-dependent continent. Consistent international development focus on Africa is often based more on donor countries' sense of solidarity and impulse to address abject poverty than on the continent's strategic, economic or geopolitical significance to donors. Aid volumes are relatively low, although consistent, (the biggest aid recipients in recent years are geopolitically strategic conflict countries), despite occasional efforts such as the UK's 'Make Poverty History' campaign, high-visibility pledges, special commissions and heart-wrenching celebrity-filled fundraising mega-events.

Most international donors have a significant presence in the least developed countries of sub-Saharan Africa. Aid provides a substantial stream of money and employment opportunities in nations characterised by decimated, corrupt and under-resourced public sectors and dysfunctional markets. African civil society's dependence on Northern funding shapes all discussion about M&E of programmes. Some of the most serious M&E issues that arise from the international aid environment concern power and accountability, clashes of results-based versus gradual change, differences in education levels and thinking patterns, oral versus text-based communication and, not least, adapting to current aid fashions.

In a donor-driven aid environment it is the donor perspective on aid that dominates – indeed, African civil society organisations (CSOs) have tended to follow Northern leads.

The Millennium Declaration and the Millennium Development Goals (MDGs), aiming to halve poverty by 2015, were adopted in 1999. Since then, three key shifts have occurred in the international aid system with a real impact on the African continent. The first involves attempts to *sys - tematise poverty reduction* efforts at the country level through mechanisms such as Poverty Reduction Strategy Papers (PRSPs), general budget support, sector-wide approaches (SWAps) and Africa's home-grown New Economic Partnership for Africa's Development (NEPAD). [29] Secondly, official donor bodies are increasingly recognising the importance of consensus-building and coordinating their roles within the aid system: the *aid effectiveness*

---

29. http://www.nepad.org

agenda. The third shift is the introduction by donors of *process conditional - ities* such as 'good governance', 'accountability' and 'transparency'. This has led to a phenomenal proliferation of African CSOs following these externally-set agendas.

Many Africans remain doubtful about whether these macro-level donor policy changes are having a positive impact on poverty levels. What primarily drives this scepticism is the fact that aid, in its different incarnations, does not seem to have brought about tangible improvements in the lives of the poorest. Indeed, the more aid-dependent African governments become, the more the poor remain disempowered and lack a voice in national policymaking. African economists point out that despite shifts to PRSPs the underlying orientation of aid is still neo-liberal and market-driven. International trading rules remain biased in favour of the status quo. Tied aid and technical assistance mean aid is used to finance the import of goods and services that could be sourced locally. Recent literature from African and international NGO (INGO) sources indicate that while there was a trend towards increased aid following the Monterrey Convention on Aid Financing in 2002 and the 'Year of Africa' 2005, much of this momentum has been lost. There is a massive gap in planned funding between what would be needed to reach the MDGs and what is likely to be provided. A July 2007 report from the UN – issued by the Secretary-General at the mid-point to the international targets' deadline – concludes bleakly that the whole of sub-Saharan Africa will fail to meet the MDGs.[30]

Comments from African participants at the workshop held in Ghana in 2005 highlighted the stumbling blocks to poverty reduction through aid:

'With increases in pledged aid, there have been corresponding increases in the conditionalities linked to aid'

'Only a limited amount of aid funds ever reach the poor'

'Aid is neither free nor value-free – e.g. the UK government continues to promote the privatisation of water and sanitation in Africa'

'There is a notable emphasis on quantity versus the quality of aid to Africa'

---

30. Millennium Development Goals Report 2007
http://www.un.org/millenniumgoals/pdf/mdg2007.pdf

'Poverty reduction seems to have taken second place globally to the 'war on terror' – with increases in military spending in both the North and the South.'

Workshop participants in Ghana in 2005 indicated that if future aid to Africa is to make a significant impact, both donors and recipients need to have a common agenda and point of departure – that of reducing poverty and putting the continent on a path to sustainable development. As one participant put it:

'Donors need to go beyond the traditional tired rhetoric of unfulfilled pledges and strategically motivated aid that currently dominates the aid industry. Recipients, on the other hand, need to ensure the efficient and prudent use of donor resources'.

INGOs in Africa: Not all rosy

Given the reality that most African-based CSOs are financially dependent on INGOs, it is important to know how African civil society regards its Northern partners. The conference in the Netherlands indicated that many harbour views which are not as rosy as many INGOs would like to believe! There are exceptions, but a significant proportion of African CSO representatives view INGOs as neo-imperialists, disproportionately controlling international aid resources and forever playing the dominant role in response to African humanitarian crises. The recent trend of INGOs to decentralise – and open offices in the South – is a significant cause of concern. African CSOs note that INGOs are thus now competing directly with home-grown organisations for resources, thus undermining the growth of an indigenous, independent African CSO sector. Furthermore, critics state that despite their rhetoric INGOs have only limited accountability mechanisms. Finally, although INGOs are leading advocates for changes in Africa, the fact that they are more accountable to their home countries than to African realities makes their involvement less urgent and locally rooted.

African CSOs and the aid architecture: any access?

Aid delivery and management in Africa has tended to be conducted as restricted official business between donors and recipient governments, to the exclusion of stakeholders such as African-based CSOs. In some instances, aid recipient governments (albeit under the influence of some liberal donors and as an afterthought) have extended a weak invitation to civil society to participate in such high-level fora as Consultative Group (CG) meetings where donors and recipient governments discuss, among other things, financial pledges for development programmes. It needs to be noted that these invitations and participation have been at the discretion of governments and that policymakers and bureaucrats routinely regard such consultation as exceptional, and not part of official norms.

The introduction of PRSPs has seen an increased rhetorical commitment to CSO participation. However, there are not many African CSOs who could take up this role – proportionately few CSOs seek to influence policy or engage in advocacy, lobbying or campaigning. Hardly any of those that do, have an advocacy remit or concentrate on issues around international aid.

Participants in Ghana offered a number of reasons for this silence from African-based CSOs. Partly, of course, there are plenty of immediate issues that need remedying to focus on locally. In part, the problem was thought to be that African CSOs generally have a limited awareness of changes in the international aid system. African civil society remains at the margins of serious national and international policy discussions. Also, CSO participation has not generally been considered important by donor coordination fora.

One of the main exceptions to this general rule relates to debt relief. Although innovative policy work that tries to articulate alternative development policy frameworks is relatively new in Africa, civil society networks on debt relief have been particularly active. There are well-established active debt-focused network organisations in Angola, Cameroon, Kenya, Mozambique, Nigeria, Senegal, Tanzania, Uganda, Zambia and Zimbabwe, some of which have had recent advocacy successes.

African CSO Policy and Advocacy

In late 2005 the INTRAC – ActionAid workshop focused on monitoring and evaluation of advocacy work in Africa. Sixty Ghanaian participants attended the first day of the four-day workshop, while representatives of over 30 more organisations from elsewhere in Africa attended the rest of the event. During the workshop, findings were presented from a three-year action research project undertaken in Brazil, Ghana, Nepal and Uganda, on planning, assessing and learning from advocacy. In each case a research facilitator worked with one or several partner organisations to delve into some of the challenges they faced with their advocacy work.[31]

In discussing CSO advocacy, it is easy to get the concepts muddled. Here, we focus on CSO monitoring and evaluation of their own advocacy work, i.e. M&E of an advocacy project. Advocacy involves arguing on behalf of a particular issue, idea or person and often goes hand in hand with campaigning and lobbying. The target of CSO advocacy is usually their home government or international development fora. Advocacy often aims to enact legislative changes in favour of the CSO's constituency – and to go beyond mere proclamations to ensure policies are implemented and have positive impacts. Some CSO advocacy targets issues around official development assistance (ODA), but most advocacy work relates to specific national-level issues such as women's empowerment or championing other rights. Some CSOs attempt to monitor government activity such as budgeting and policy – M&E of government.

The issue of policy and advocacy was chosen as the basis for the M&E workshop in Ghana because advocacy is especially problematic in Africa, where the culture of challenging authority is generally speaking weak.

One of the African CSOs with a policy focus is the Zimbabwe-based African Forum and Network on Debt and Development (AFRODAD).[32] Most CSOs, however, have limited capacity for constructive engagement in efforts to reform the international aid system. Until recently, Northern NGOs considered civil society-based policy work on alternative development frameworks to be too political to allow consideration of financial support. Creating development knowledge, policies and programming models was, until recently, the exclusive preserve of governments and international development partners, especially multilateral agencies. Most African CSOs don't possess the in-depth knowledge, resources and contacts needed to engage at this level, especially since it is very difficult to make oneself heard in official processes. It is partly because of African CSOs' lack

---

31. The workshop was facilitated by Jenny Chapman, of ActionAid with the support of Sarah Okwaare (ActionAid Uganda) and Vincent Azumah (ActionAid Ghana).

32. www.afrodad.org

of capacity to engage in policy work that INGOs are now emerging as 'alternative voices' on poverty reduction strategies in Africa.

Even when an African CSO clearly has good ideas and thought-through plans for lobbying and advocacy, funding is far from guaranteed. Neither official donors nor INGOs are keen to fund Southern participation in the aid debate, despite the current attention given to the topic. Donor NGOs are reluctant to fund a programme which does not fit with their current priorities. When the debt relief campaign was in vogue, and being prioritised by most INGOs, they were prepared to fund Southern CSOs to participate. They did so only because debt relief was on top of the current agenda. When INGOs shifted advocacy and lobbying priorities from debt relief to trade, most African CSOs were obliged to follow suit. This was despite the fact that the debt crisis remained unresolved and critically important and programmes to support Heavily Indebted Poor Countries (HIPCs) were not achieving anticipated results. In Africa the effort to keep the debt campaign alive was led by a small group of dedicated CSOs, but at great financial cost.

Policy and Advocacy: Capacity Building Priorities

The argument for supporting African CSOs to develop and sustain rigorous engagement in pro-poor policy work cannot be repeated too often. Both African CSOs and Northern INGOs play an important role as independent watchdogs monitoring the actions of government. It is critically important that they have the skills for the effective implementation, monitoring and evaluation of aid projects/programmes. Through budget tracking and advocacy-type projects, many African CSOs can also help ensure that African governments adhere to the values of accountability and poverty targeting whose rhetoric underpins the MDGs. In the literature, specific reference is made to the Tanzania Independent Monitoring Group (IMG)[33] which is reported to have 'contributed to a positive swing in (aid) relations, characterised by increased country ownership, more responsiveness by international partners to improving their policies and practices; greater transparency in the dialogue process, and increased effective use of aid ' (Mwakasege 2005). Such a body is an example of good practice in monitoring government behaviour.

---

33. www.tzdpg.or.tz

The key question for CSOs involved in policy and advocacy activities is 'what kinds of M&E mechanisms are best for assessing our effect on aid recipient governments?' The answer is far from straightforward. At the Ghana workshop, one session was called 'How can you know whether you have really made a difference?' This session raised a number of very challenging questions that the workshop did not have time to address:

- Can you say your advocacy work was successful even if your campaigners end up in prison? Or if the bill you are working on is scrapped?
- Is it enough for ministers just to read your bill?
- Is the amount of 'heat' or anger you generate an indicator of change?
- Does a backlash show that your strategy is the right one?
- With work on gender relations there is no easily identifiable target – there are no communities of abusers. How then do you assess how far you are achieving your aims?

In terms of M&E of advocacy, one key observation was that there is often a push to look for big, dramatic changes. However, much advocacy work takes years or even decades to begin to show significant advances. Workshop participants stressed that we need to pay attention to smaller changes at the grassroots level as well, and observe, record and value them.

Since the workshop's theme was M&E of advocacy, it follows that this topic is fairly prominent. However, although advocacy is quite abstract and hence difficult to monitor, CSOs with other areas of activity also face pressing challenges in monitoring and evaluating their work effectively and constructively. Issues of power and accountability, critical thinking and M&E methods or tools featured strongly in many of the discussions. A specifically African issue was the relative importance of the written versus the spoken word in M&E. These and other topics are discussed below.

Thorny M&E issues: whose is the power and voice?

Power relations, accountability and real change

Power relations shape M&E directly. The decisions of what to monitor, and the evaluation of whether an activity has been successful or not, hold the key to how a development intervention is perceived by all those stake-holders who were not directly involved. Monitoring determines what is considered important in an intervention, something that can vary drastically depending on whom you ask. The 'blueprint versus learning' question is key: the tension between financially and practically accounting for project outputs, and between recording and analysing the subtle human-level changes that have taken place. The stereotype is of the back-donor requiring stark numerical data, and the implementers trying to convey the complex effects on the ground. Hence, the design and implementation of M&E is a direct reflection of who calls the shots in the project – whose accountability to whom takes priority.

The following experiences in Africa (by international as well as African organisations) are examples of how CSOs grapple with complex issues regarding power and M&E. This includes the donor-implementer power dynamics, facilitator-organisation relations, identifying power structures for advocacy and change work, and working with existing community power relations. In many cases, the power relationships discussed here in relation to M&E issues underpin the other aspects of a development activity as well.

Power and Downward Accountability

The balancing act of being accountable both to your funders and your stakeholders who are not providing money 'underlies [many M&E tensions] and the question must be solved', as an MS Denmark development veteran expressed it at the sixth evaluation conference. A participant with a donor NGO perspective pointed out the problem: how can you extract meaning and draw conclusions about the effect you are having, when you are faced with reports and information from hundreds of in-country projects? Hiring external evaluators doesn't necessarily help: commissioning and following up consultants' work sometimes just means more, possibly unnecessary, paperwork. The sheer workload at the funder INGO level necessarily means simplifying and extracting key data. The more implementers are accountable upwards, the more this hard data approach dominates their M&E. The subtler points of learning from evaluations perhaps needs to be appreciated and used at a different level or section of NGO management, but as the 'learning versus accountability' debate has considered at length, this is rarely a priority.

While the funders struggle to keep up with data flooding in from projects, the opposite is the case at the grassroots level: typically, little or any learning or data is fed back to the supposed beneficiaries of the project, whose input has been used to collate information for the M&E report. Conference participants mentioned a 'near-conspiracy situation' whereby hardly any research, censuses, monitoring and mapping results are fed back to the people who have engaged with evaluators and taken time to provide information. It becomes easy for ordinary people to dismiss research and monitoring as pointless if they never see the developmental returns from it. This reiterates the crucial importance of downward accountability.

Different untypical accountability relationships were discussed during the conference session. For example, a Ghanaian and an Irish participant spoke in favour of beneficiaries evaluating the NGO running a project – downward accountability in practice. Demanding contractual compliance (in terms of transparency and accountability) from donors as well was one suggestion. 'Lateral' accountability – to organisations you aren't working with directly (peer reviews) could improve quality immensely. In a peer review, staff from other organisations in a similar position to yours – but who have not been involved with the project – evaluate your work. Participants said that peer reviews are 'scary but effective'. A Spanish participant described her experience of peer evaluation, pointing out that it makes it difficult to disseminate the evaluation report as it ends up containing many sensitive areas of information. This raises the perennial question about how genuine INGOs' professed willingness to submit themselves to scrutiny really is. A Dutch participant asked how serious top INGO officials really are about utilising M&E findings.

Donor priorities shaping M&E

The questions about donor NGOs' sincerity about being scrutinised had been discussed previously at the Ghana workshop. A participant who had evaluated Oxfam's community peace building project in Rwanda described their experience of monitoring a project, describing the difficulty of verifying the information you get. The project had aimed at combating gender inequality by putting non-literate women at the centre of decision-making processes about initiatives that could help consolidate peace in communities. The data that had been gathered pointed towards very positive outcomes in terms of the gender equality aspects of the project. Despite this, however, the evaluation team remained sceptical that such radical changes could have occurred with only a few weeks' training and awareness-raising. Their interpretation was that villagers had obviously realised that Oxfam's goal, underlying peace-building, was gender relations, and were giving the evaluators the information they wanted to hear to ensure that the project continued to be funded.

In an attempt to find other ways of verifying the collected information, the workshop participant proposed that staff could try asking for observations from 'insider-outsiders' i.e. people who, for a variety of reasons, might be regular visitors to the community – government agricultural extension workers for example. A mixture of internal and external people in any evaluation team could help generate critical discussion of stories. One strategy, used by World Vision in the monitoring of some of its project work, is to ask village leaders and their advisors to observe whether or not change is taking place. This produces a particularly charged dynamic when World Vision is raising grassroots awareness of the need to abolish or modify harmful traditional practices.

Another suggestion was to question children in the community and get them to talk about what they see at home or in the community through role-play and other participatory methods. At this point, however, other participants pointed out that if a project is really bad, people tell you so, and do not bother to tell you what you want to hear!

Monitoring and evaluating progress on an advocacy project challenging child trafficking in Togo raised some interesting M&E questions. Attitudes towards child trafficking had been changing radically in Togo: once a non-issue, it had become a popular topic of NGO discussion. The project's M&E involved using some statistical data to see whether trafficking had diminished – e.g. looking at whether child enrolment rates have increased at school. But other measures are also seen as positive indicators of change – such as the extent to which people are talking about trafficking (sending children off to the cities is culturally acceptable, so a change in the use of words to describe the practice could mean there has been an attitude shift). The number of other organisations in Togo that have started working on the issue could also be seen as an indicator of a shift in attitude – or, more cynically, as a reflection of the increasing popularity and 'fashion' of child trafficking, and the commensurate increase in funding availability. When this particular organisation first started advocating to end the practice, people didn't consider it a problem.

Facilitator power

One participant at the Ghana workshop discussed the pivotal role of facilitators. Facilitators working with communities to assess ongoing advocacy invariably play a political role for the facilitator cannot be neutral. S/he must bring in new ideas when encouraging learning from and assessment of advocacy. While facilitators can act as a catalyst for change, prematurely introducing new ideas when an organisation is not ready to receive them, this can be disempowering and/or spark resistance. It is therefore the responsibility of the facilitator to think carefully about when and how to introduce tools – to undertake a mini-contextual analysis. Facilitators should not accept and use tools without analysing context and power and without self-reflectively analysing their own thinking and motivations in introducing them.

One speaker gave a warning example about the way in which a facilitator's own value system can impact negatively on the way an assessment and learning tool is introduced. Someone without adequate political consciousness, commitment or training can misuse a tool and cause harm. Here she was referring to the use of ActionAid gender tools (such as Stepping Stones and REFLECT) that do not necessarily facilitate analysis of power and gender and can oversimplify social situations through a focus on peaceful resolution of conflict. The question asked was, 'is the facilitator in the right position to stimulate others to think critically?'

Advocacy-specific questions of power: Focus on legal and political changes

At the Ghana workshop, participants discussed how it is possible to actually know that you have made a difference. They noted the tendency to focus almost solely on legal and political changes when assessing advocacy work, and to monitor campaigning activities, such as the number of marches, rallies and demonstrations. This type of focus can skew the M&E of advocacy work as well as the activities of the campaign itself. Changes in legislation don't necessarily create any change at the grassroots. A participant said that one way they knew that their advocacy work was being effective, was when the numbers of people involved in their marches increased. However, in another session participants noted that this is not necessarily a valid indicator: for those who take part in marches may not be aware of the objectives of the organisers. They may have been encouraged to demonstrate without knowing why. Lessons from group work indicated that the most powerful advocacy was that which was clearly linked back to constituencies.

The question of power dynamics within advocacy work was stressed by the facilitators throughout the Ghana workshop. Above all, it was emphasised that advocacy initiatives cannot be analysed until questions of power have been understood. This is why the last day of the workshop involved a session on power, and understanding how it can variously manifest itself.

The difficulty of assessing advocacy was further stressed by the fact that even achieving policy change is not necessarily a measure of broader change in people's lives. You can monitor the progression of a bill through to becoming an act of parliament, but its implementation, enforcement and impact are what really matters. The real-life impact of advocacy invariably rests on wider goals of empowerment and creation of democratic public space.

The importance of analysing existing power dynamics was raised at the sixth evaluation conference as well. A participant from Zambia raised the issue of accountability within African communities, especially the cultural difficulties of challenging senior people. This makes it hard to demand accountability from e.g. board members who are probably influential figures in the community. The chair of the session brought the discussion back to the community level, pointing out that work is needed to allow mutual accountability, trust and ownership to grow within communities as well as between NGOs and communities.

Tools: the great distraction

Mentioning M&E tools – the exercises, analytical methods and interview techniques of M&E – always raise great hopes. Although the basic methods for M&E are widely known and flexible, M&E events are often seen as occasions for learning new and exciting tools and exercises.

Workshop facilitators in Ghana pointed out that discussions turned to tools and methods whenever the matter of assessing change was raised. It seems that the idea of new tools can often become a mental crutch that people lean on and assume that they need. This could be because it's more exciting to engage with learning a new tool than grappling with making sense of the world using tried and tested methods. As such, new tools are not necessarily conducive to learning. For the ActionAid researchers preparing the ground for the Ghana workshop, the key to using tools is ensuring that they are combined with critical thinking, are participatory and are able to tease out power and gender dynamics.

Similarly, people get obsessed with thinking about indicators and overwhelm themselves with an unmanageable number of them. Problems occur when indicators become overcomplicated. It is an accepted 'rule of thumb' that the more elaborate the M&E design, the less likely it is to be used in practice.

In discussions after a session on the use of tools, one commentator noted that M&E tools cannot be divorced from the reality in which they are used. When they are imposed from outside they can be influenced by the politics of the donor. This also diminishes the commitment of those who are supposed to be using the tool. There is a tendency amongst organisations to accept the tools that they are handed down from above without necessarily being convinced of their merits or sometimes without fully mastering their use. Staff might not feel able to use the tools they are being given, but at the same time don't feel able to complain about them. When people haven't seen the underlying logic of a tool, they tend to resist using it. Many M&E tools are thus considered to stifle local innovation.

Another common problem is that there is a great deal of mystery surrounding M&E and people feel alienated because of the complicated jargon involved. This is hard to avoid, however, as the jargon is so widespread. Furthermore, staff believe that M&E is something that can only be done by experts from outside. This helps to explain why participants were hoping to be given the 'perfect tool' that would enable them to fulfil their donor's requirements for ongoing monitoring or impact assessment.

Another strategy for assessing progress is the use of exchange visits. This isn't just about helping people formulate policy, but was described as a 'powerful monitoring tool'. It was used very successfully by the ActionAid research teams in Uganda and Brazil. It encourages critical thinking, as it leads people to make comparisons between their own work and that of others, and to think through how strategies used in a foreign context might play out in their own.

The most important tool: critical thinking

At the start of ActionAid's four-country action research project on monitoring advocacy, the intended focus had been on 'developing innovative tools and methodologies with which to assess the impact of people-centred advocacy.' However, as it progressed, a number of other critical factors started to emerge, spurring a shift in focus away from the discovery of such magic bullets. There was a gradual realisation that 'innovative M&E tools' are not as essential for assessing advocacy projects as had been anticipated. Rather, the emphasis is on how these tools are used to encourage in-depth discussion and analysis. This was followed by awareness that critical thinking, rather than any specific method, is perhaps the most important 'tool' needed for the effective assessment of advocacy campaigns. During the research, those involved realised – belatedly – that advocacy campaigns are ongoing processes which could benefit greatly from cycles of critical analysis of planning, action assessment and learning. Finally, there was widespread agreement that it is very important to assess changes in advocacy campaigns by making note of shifts in power and gender relations within the target community.

Most of the examples in this section came from the Ghana workshop on M&E of advocacy. Some of the key challenges organisations had faced when trying to monitor advocacy processes include:

Contextual Analysis – real power dynamics

Using critical thinking and power analysis when planning advocacy work will broaden understanding of where change can happen, and the arenas or levels where you can aim to change power dynamics. Advocacy work should not be limited to the policy or legislative level. One proposed strategy was advocacy within the informal authority structures (especially traditional authorities) that dominate Africa, as well as the obvious more formal ones. Not taking such authorities into account had presented great challenges both for monitoring changes in customary law, and for the extent to which changes in national level legislation could influence the attitudes and behaviours of traditional bodies.

Confusion over the end goal

There was a tendency among some workshop participants to gloss over difficult questions about the ultimate end goal of their advocacy work. For instance, a number of organisations represented at the meeting claimed to be working on gender issues, particularly on violence against women. However, their strategies frequently involve the use of mediation: bringing together the survivor and perpetrator of violence. Such methods may gloss over the problem, apparently achieving community harmony, but actually failing to address issues of gender equality. The anti-violence message was often presented through Biblical teaching – i.e. that men should love their wives. However, that approach does not address issues of power, in particular the predominance of patriarchal attitudes towards women embodied by traditional leaders and, indeed, the Church. Although these groups were using the rhetoric of women's rights, in practice their focus did not have a rights base. If you're not clear about your aims, it becomes even more difficult to assess the impact of your work.

How does change really happen?

In order to measure change, there must be an understanding both of the end goal of the advocacy initiative and of the steps that can demonstrate that change towards that end goal is taking place. Knowing this in advance of the project is not always straightforward. Hence, it is important to be as clear as possible, and keep up a continuing process of critical reflection to realign the advocacy work and keep it on track. Which tools to use in order to assess change will depend on the context. What is important is how these tools are used – they should not be employed in a mechanical and unthinking manner. It is vital to remain aware of both their strengths and weaknesses. It was suggested to workshop participants that when they are doing assessments they should continually question the information they had been given, asking 'who, what, why and when'.

One example given by the ActionAid researchers was adapting the use of timelines in Nepal to make them more useful for ongoing planning and learning from advocacy work. The timeline can be used as a way of recording an organisation's history, or the steps taken to date in a campaign, without any further analysis. However, by adding critical questions to it, such as why a particular strategy had been chosen, who was involved, what kind of impact it had had and how the changing context was affecting their work, what had previously been a descriptive tool became a more dynamic instrument for learning and developing future strategies.

The discussions on methods and analysis are a good example of how much easier it is to get distracted by details than to address fundamental issues in our work. Often, M&E can go wrong because the project/programme it is meant to assess is itself unfocused or insufficiently thought-through. Another pitfall is creating elaborate M&E systems when it is not clear what information is sought, and for what reason. Focusing too much on M&E details and methods can also distract us from using M&E results most productively in order to learn and improve practice. In development as in everything else, it is always simpler to deal with a solid, well-understood and coherent process, where the ability to think critically about your work is key.

Documentation, writing and oral culture

The conflict between formal and informal, mechanic and fluid, anecdotal and statistical M&E emerged in a though-provoking and energetic session at the sixth evaluation conference about documentation, writing and Africa. The discussion about recording and reporting M&E data in written form showed just how dominant, yet alien, the standard Northern patterns of behaviour can be when applied to the field of development.

Africa is a continent with many rich cultures underpinned by recitation, listening and memorising and which have survived without being written down. At the sixth evaluation conference, a Kenyan representative pointed out that 'writing came to us with a caution' – early African experiences of text and signatures on paper often proved to be contracts signing away land rights to outsiders. The difference between the emphasis on paper versus the emphasis on spoken communication goes deeper than just documenting methods, but includes whole ways of thinking and working. Several INGOs working in Africa reported that their African contacts had a tendency to provide good, insightful analysis in speech, but to only

The discord between narrative and formal M&E approaches

describe activities in writing.

At the Ghana workshop, the problem of documentation was raised repeatedly. A number of reasons were put forward to explain the weakness of written recording:

- Many Africans have not acquired the culture of painstakingly documenting events and therefore can regard such a process as alien.

- Resistance to the formal documentation process may have come about as a result of Africans feeling they are 'judged' or 'pigeonholed' by the nature of the documents they submit.

- Local CSOs don't always understand the rationale behind their own documentation (which they primarily prepare for donors) and so may not necessarily even able to explain it to the people they work with.

- Documenting work can be draining, especially if it is based on numerical indicators.

In response to these problems, some solutions were put forward. There was a feeling that African CSOs, like those elsewhere, would like to find their own way of recording their work, possibly based on the storytelling tradition. This could mean using audio or video and/or using drama or song. It was also suggested that these ways of recording change could be more informal when you start engaging at the community level. Over the long term, once trust is established, these could be formalised.

To clarify the concepts, we should stress that by 'stories' we do not mean imagined fairytales, but anecdotes, analogies and personal explanations of change that do not necessarily conform to linear cause-effect descriptions. Workshop participants identified some key problems with storytelling – there has to be some critical thinking involved in order to draw out the core of the story. Some elements of the story may be obvious to the narrator, but not necessarily to the listener. Stories can also be interpreted in different ways. They will often have a moral, but the way this moral is understood will change according to a number of factors, in particular age and cultural background.

At the Ghanaian workshop, a participant said 'We clearly have something to say, but oral approaches are being sidelined, are not documented or acknowledged, and are looked down upon. There is clearly "apartheid of knowledge" between written and oral narratives.' At the sixth evaluation conference, an African activist participant pointed out that there is wide scope for practical applications, learning and ownership from the story approach. There is clearly a disparity between these two approaches – and a key question for INTRAC is whether the twain can ever meet.

So how can we build a feedback system, with monitoring and reporting, based on an oral system? Participants at the sixth evaluation conference had several strong and innovative suggestions.

Most Significant Change methodology is seen as a positive method of 'appreciative enquiry', which incorporates storytelling ideas to try to document processes. Storytelling – as a means of conveying information – is becoming an extensively used tool in South Africa, according to CDRA, the South African organisational development NGO. Storytelling has been around in M&E for a long time, but always under the 'anecdotal' umbrella. The biggest problem is confusion over long-term scientific scope, where you have to provide large samples to give evidence of changes. Mostly people are not satisfied by a rough picture with descriptions of changes. For added weight you would not just use one or two stories, but a range in order to allow patterns to emerge.

Outcome mapping might be a useful method to help to do so. It charts attitudinal and behavioural change. It may be the 'weakest' part of an evaluation but it is useful for monitoring since it is not very rigid, but contains a range of indicators nonetheless.

Participants at the sixth evaluation conference also mentioned other innovative oral monitoring methods. One participant suggested using mobile phones and talk-back radio shows as a monitoring tool. If the radio presenter asks for feedback on a development initiative, people can easily phone in to the live radio show and offer their views – some clear indication of people's views would come out immediately, strongly – and transparently. A speaker from Ghana also spoke in favour of using the media to disseminate monitoring results. A South African development consultant mentioned that in a project in Lesotho, women's immediate and informal feedback turned out to be a useful indicator: their laughter and heckling from the fringes of a meeting circle when they did not agree with progress reports must be taken seriously. He also described how the mayor of a town had commissioned a choral competition to provide a musical report on a development project. One participant had an experience of using forum theatre in Uganda for involving people and acting out recommendations.

Some would argue that Africa needs to be regarded as a 'special case' because of not being immersed in the 'developed' world's habit of using the written word. This was discussed in more detail by a participant from Zimbabwe: there is an assumption that 'there is no science in Africa'. Since written text is the medium of the powerful, Africa is disadvantaged by inability to write clearly, thus further alienating Africans from the global development environment.

However, is there not something patronising about assuming that Africans need special treatment because they are less confident in using mainstream systems? We all know that many formal education systems in Africa are in crisis and it is universally accepted that everyone should be able to learn to write, read, use information technology and analyse the world objectively. However, this does not mean that 'hard science', numbers, statistics, formulae and complicated English-language reports should be given greater value than commonsensical evaluation based on everyday observation and stories about trends and patterns. There is a strong sense that legitimising and appreciating oral narratives in M&E shifts accountability 'downstream', towards the beneficiaries, whose language it uses, rather than that of the funders.

There was some concern that storytelling-type evidence would tend to analyse the activities level rather than more abstract impacts. However, as with conventional M&E, this depends on the astuteness of the informants and the questions asked. Ideally, it should be possible to use formal science and writing without losing the richness of the oral tradition. A combination of these has been used in South Africa, where a widespread civic movement has managed to shift a civil society has successfully challenged senior politicians' misperceptions about the HIV pandemic and secured wider entitlements to antiretroviral therapy (ART). CDRA, a participant at the sixth evaluation conference, played a seminal part in the campaign, using a combination of story and scientific methods.

CASE STUDY *Santa Yallah Society – Central River Province, the Gambia*

APSO, the former Irish development worker service, has shown how oral dissemination in M&E reporting can lead to empowerment and action. In 1999 APSO commenced a capacity building initiative with four Gambian CBOs. Most members of one of them, the Santa Yallah Society, are female rice farmers. One of their activities is a ferry service to an island where members have rice fields. The organisation had bought two boats with a small grant from CIDA, the Canadian international development agency. Fees charged to passengers were designed to cover fuel and maintenance costs and to help repay the loan. APSO sent an Irish development worker to carry out an organisational needs assessment. A speaker of Mandinka, the predominant local language, he stayed in the area for a week, visiting members in their villages, meeting other locally-based community development workers and key people. His assessment, written in English and sent to the CBO management committee, analysed their organisational strengths and weaknesses and looked at how the income earned from the boat service was managed. The volume of passenger traffic and the income which should have been raised from fees suggested that the original loan ought to have been repaid. In fact, this was far from the case. In the absence of effective financial management systems, it was very hard to identify exactly what had occurred.

Time passed, but without a reaction to the report. APSO decided to convert its findings into a format which could be used by the wider membership of Santa Yallah. Translated into Mandinka and Wolof, the other local languages, it was put onto cassette tapes given to the Santa Yallah management committee and played at membersí public meetings. While APSO staff were considering their next move dramatic news came: the predominantly female membership of Santa Yallah had replaced the management committee. The new committee got in touch with APSO and they resumed work to jointly develop an plan to manage the ferries as well as to develop a wider plan to be taken go other would-be partners/donors.

This vignette shows how people can be empowered to take action when they have access to information in forms they can relate to. The key stakeholders, the members, were reached, at modest cost, by audio tapes in their own languages. The key lesson learned is that the use of a lingua franca, in this case English, can be extremely disempowering for those who lack fluency.

Informal and ongoing observation vs the 'M&E mystique'

It makes sense to keep track of how your project is going without writing down every single observation – but where does this kind of informal assessment join up with formal monitoring? Many workshop participants in Ghana saw M&E as a separate, discrete process to informal ongoing assessment, rather than considering them linked. The 'apartheid of knowledge' surfaces when informal observations are not documented and are thus devalued. The more M&E is seen as an alien exercise – undertaken by English-speaking foreigners using strange methods and coming to abstract conclusions – the more it is removed from productive learning and Southern capacity development.

Comments by some participants in Ghana uncovered a perceptual divide between the idea of formal M&E and the type of ongoing reflection that people undertake routinely. Most participants were able to identify changes they saw in attitudes and power dynamics at community level. However, this information was generally based on *ad hoc* observation and was rarely formally documented. Perhaps participants felt these types of observations are too 'obvious' to warrant committing to paper. They also noted the lesser emphasis of the written tradition in Africa. Yet, previous lessons from ActionAid research on advocacy M&E suggest that keeping a written, central record of events, decisions made at meetings, and notes of changes that seem to be appearing as a result, significantly improves strategic planning.

One issue that became apparent in Ghana workshop discussions was that many organisations don't know how to undertake systematic M&E

and are in fact reluctant to do any. Staff may document and report on only visible outputs or may borrow tools and indicators from other organisations without thinking whether they are contextually appropriate. As one participant put it, M&E processes seems 'huge and unmanageable' and staff just want a way of getting through it. Assessment tends to be a donor requirement and finding ways to actually learn from advocacy work appears to be a very new concept. Informal assessment goes on all the time, but people don't always document what they see happening, nor necessarily look for the lessons they can learn from it.

The feeling that M&E is a hard science, not something that ordinary staff can do, emerged in a discussion about novel indicators. The Ghana workshop participants discussed local indicators that can be developed in a participatory manner and counter the widespread impression that indicators are imposed from above. One such example provoked discussion about whether locally-created indicators would be 'scientific' enough.

Villagers who had been involved in a food security project decided that one indicator of improvements would be the number of people keeping dogs, and whether the dogs' ribs were showing. While some participants felt this was a positive example of finding locally appropriate measures of change, others disputed it, for better-off families might be more likely to keep dogs. However, the 'hungry dog' indicator is interesting because it is based on a simple observation.

Other participants gave equally striking – albeit anecdotal – examples of observations which suggested that their work had made a difference. One participant's idea of attitudinal change in gender relations was that husbands would now 'beg' their wives for sex, rather than use force. One might question, however, whether this is an indicator of fundamental changes in intra-household power.

At the sixth evaluation conference several African participants had encouraging examples of how to develop M&E techniques 'for local consumption'. Many involved embedding indicators in ongoing work, involving partners in participatory indicator-setting, and fostering long-term relationships.

CASE STUDY *MS – Ongoing, Visual Monitoring*

African country offices of Mellemfolkeligt Samvirke – MS, the Danish Association for International Co-operation – use the Most Significant Change methodology to extract evaluation points from their embedded monitoring systems. MS offices use quarterly monitoring charts (QMCs) for their partner organisations, to keep track of their aims, planned activities and implementation progress. The QMC system was developed in response to a weakness in monitoring systems, aiming to make monitoring more accessible and relevant. The QMC has columns for expected and actual achievements and expected and actual changes. Over the course of the quarter, staff fill in 'expected' and 'actual' outcomes for each objective. The charts are on public view near the entrance to the office. At the end of the year, it is fairly easy to get an overview of progress from the year's four QMCs. The organisation invites MS, stakeholders and officials to a meeting where everyone works through the charts to discuss trends and interesting points, an engaging exercise that stakeholders and communities find interesting. Adding significant information to the 'comments' column of the QMC is a way to elaborate on progress in an interactive way.

Managers in the different partner organisations have been very pleased with the QMC system, although staff have had a harder time facing up to the increased transparency that comes with writing actual achievements directly next to the intended achievements. The QMC system makes sure that monitoring is linked directly to planning. Finally, the following year's plans are drawn up, using the past QMCs as a guide.

Since the information for the QMCs is needed for everyday work, it makes sure that monitoring data is recorded even without an elaborate separate M&E system. One of the weaknesses of the QMCs is that the recorded changes often stay at the 'activities' level, rather than capturing impacts.

Adan Wario Kabelo, Programme Development Officer at MS Kenya, describes the QMC as follows: 'A successful monitoring system starts from explicit planning. Before monitoring takes place, there has to be a plan so that it's the execution of the plan that is being monitored ... It is imperative that we know whether we have achieved what we intended to achieve and whether our actions/activities are leading us to the desired situation. Without a clear direction it's true that 'you cannot get lost if you do not know where you are going'.

The system hinges on the existence of a clear plan and links the agreed objectives to the activities and to the intended or unintended results and thus provides room for reflection. During annual reviews participants can rapidly review performance against annual plans. The QMC is a tool which can update management on what has been achieved in the previous quarter and enable them to advise on future plans.

These examples show that M&E does not always need to be the preserve of outside experts, the impression that is generally given. The sense that M&E is 'not for us' reinforces the impression of development as an alien concept. If CSOs are not thinking through the course and intended effect of their programmes, if NGOs spring up in response to swings in donor trends, if monitoring is something done reluctantly as a donor requirement and if there is little awareness of how to learn from M&E, then it is imperative that we demand devolved and decentralised power in the aid chain. We must focus on keeping M&E simple and grounded and advocate for vernacular interpretations of reality.

Conclusion

The African experience of M&E from INTRAC's workshop in Ghana and sixth evaluation conference brings home the scale of the gap between development rhetoric and reality. This chapter has noted the stark reality that Africa is highly aid dependent, which means that the aid industry is a viable and well-paid sector on a par with government and business when it comes to employment opportunities for the well-educated.

Partly because of this, and partly because of global power and economic relations, African NGOs and other CSOs have very little bargaining power in setting the agenda for aid work. At times, it seems like African NGOs spend all their capacity for innovation and adaptability on reorienting themselves to new aid trends, leaving little scope to deepen and improve their anti-poverty work. As a result, ownership, 'buy-in', learning and sustainability levels can be very low. There is an enormous gap between everyday communication and formal English reporting and a pseudo-occult status attached to Western M&E methods and practitioners, and the emphasis on keeping exhaustive written records. Reliance on a foreign way of thinking that sits uncomfortably with the way Africans would normally go about things is a constant undercurrent in the discussions and experiences of African M&E practitioners.

The message they send is loud and clear: there is not enough accountability downwards, accountability of development practitioners to those they are supposed to serve. Current M&E practices show whose 'reality' is valued and whose interpretation of events is the accepted one – and all too often, M&E experience shows that is the donor – be they bilateral or INGO – who are the real power-holders.

Uncomplicated, common-sense M&E that is built into programme activities is the way forward. M&E systems should be based on a few, thoughtfully selected indicators. When gathering data, there should be space for people's own interpretations and narratives about events. Most importantly, M&E results should always 'close the loop' and be presented back to the intervention's stakeholders. There are plenty of easy, innovative ways of doing so – through common sense, clear thinking and understanding your context, with some help from selected tools.

Despite all this pessimism, the impression African development practitioners gave at the sixth evaluation conference was one of energy, determination and innovation. Many of them already use oral narrative and locally-determined indicators in their work. They have refused to be intimidated by alien external formats. As long as there are more such vocal and insightful African M&E practitioners, the future looks positive.

3

Asia

Esther Mebrahtu

Rethinking International Cooperation from an Asian Perspective

This chapter presents the ideas and concerns of Asian participants at the sixth evaluation conference and the preceding New Delhi workshop convened by INTRAC and by Participatory Research in Asia (PRIA), a Delhi-based centre for promoting learning, participation and democratic governance.[34] The workshop[35] discussed participatory M&E and its application, different methodologies, key issues and problems emerging from practice and potential areas for future knowledge generation.[36]

This chapter also draws on background research undertaken for the workshop convened by the Overseas Development Institute (ODI) entitled 'Southern Voices for Change in the International Aid Architecture'. It:

- highlights Asian voices on the current reform of the aid architecture (in particular changes in aid delivery systems and types of aid)

---

34. www.pria.org

35. The workshop had 48 participants from Afghanistan, Bangladesh, India, Nepal, New Zealand, the Netherlands, Pakistan, the UK and Vietnam.

36. The speakers' papers can be downloaded at
www.intrac.org/pages/PRIAWorkshop.html

- assesses the degree of civil society participation within this reform process
- assesses the impact of these changes on M&E practice, most specifically within three key areas of the activities of civil society organisations (CSOs) – networks/forums; advocacy and policy initiatives and relief and rehabilitation projects.

Given the heterogeneity of the region, there is obviously no one 'Asian perspective' on these issues. The discussion therefore places greater emphasis on the views of a sample of low and middle income Asian countries which have relatively 'high' levels of aid – including Bangladesh, India, Pakistan, the Philippines, Sri Lanka and Afghanistan. It is also important to acknowledge from the outset that there are vast differences in levels of civil society development across the region. In countries such as Bangladesh and India NGOs are very well-established and at the forefront of debates and approaches to M&E, capacity building and related issues. In other countries such as Afghanistan, however, NGOs and CSOs are not well established and/or face multiple constraints.

Asian civil society has spoken out on issues of aid reform but the range of regional contributions to available literature, especially from local CSOs, is limited in comparison with material produced by Northern academic centres, CSOs and institutes. This is hardly surprising given the biased construct of the aid system and highly unbalanced power relations between donors and recipient states. However, with the obvious exceptions of such large high-profile NGOs as BRAC and PROSHIKA, this imbalance also reflects the insufficient capacity of most Asian CSOs to effectively engage in high-level policy discourse. The literature which does exist however is extremely varied in scope – making it difficult to summarise in any meaningful way. Hence, we attempt to simply categorise and interpret the key generic trends identified.

General Trend 1: Trade not Aid

Possibly the most notable trend identified by the literature review prepared by Debapriya Bhattacharya for the ODI workshop *Asian Perspectives on Aid Architecture* (Bhattacharya 2005) relates to the recent marked emphasis on the role of international trade systems in poverty reduction efforts in Asia. Middle- and some low-income Asian states are currently experiencing many structural changes prompted by accelerating economic growth and the increasing role of international trade in their economies. The bulk of foreign exchange inflows is through export receipts and expatriate remittances, rather than foreign aid. This trend has led to a shift in the focus of development thinking in South and South East Asia away from foreign aid to issues relating to the export of goods and services. Consequently, Asian CSOs are less engaged with foreign aid issues than they were in the 1990s.

Local CSOs quoted in Bhattacharya's study hastened to point out the apparent lack of coherence between the aid and trade policies of governments. They illustrated this point by citing the examples of Norway and USA.

'Norway, although a generous donor when it comes to aid, is ranked tenth because of its protectionist trade policies. Conversely, the USA scores well on trade (even though it ensures that it penalises countries through tariff and non-tariff barriers), but badly on everything else and is, therefore, ranked low in the aid league table'

(Tujan, 2005:3).

General Trend 2: Aid and the Security Agenda

Many workshop discussions supported the widespread concern in Asia, expressed in the literature, about the nexus between aid and the security agenda of Northern donors. Tujan argues that Asia – the major focus on the war on terror – has been particularly affected as donors such as the USA and Japan shift their aid strategies to accommodate their regional geopolitical interests (Tujan, 2005b). Pakistan, for example, has moved from being 14th on the list of aid-recipient countries in 1999/2000 to first place in 2001/02. According to statistics from the Organisation for Economic Cooperation and Development (OECD), Pakistan remains at the top end of the list, along with Iraq and Afghanistan. Regarding Latin America, Asian CSOs view with suspicion efforts by the US to provide assistance to Colombia in the war against drugs (Dàvila, 2005).

General Trend 3: Direct Budget Support and Tied Aid

An interesting finding of the Delhi workshop was the extent to which Asian NGOs emphasised the inverse nature of the relationship between aid conditionalities imposed by donors and genuine country ownership. They argued that it is insufficiently acknowledged that conditionality creates unequal aid relationships and that genuine country ownership can only be promoted through allowing flexibility in the policy process. Asian workshop participants made an interesting distinction between the *process and content* of aid conditionality. Although content tends to be heavily criticised, they felt that if donors were more discriminating when giving aid, the need for conditionality would decrease.

Very closely linked to this discussion was the participants' general ambivalence over the benefits of direct budget support[37] as a way to release aid funds. There were concerns that this could lead to a misuse of funds and that the shift to programme aid places a much greater administrative strain on governments as 'it is essentially a management-intensive approach' (see Bakewell, 2003). Capacity development and enhanced governance were therefore considered to be essential requirements for both donors and recipients.

While participants stated that Asian CSOs are now receiving greater funds than ever before, they were concerned that in a donor-driven aid system civil society voices and proposals are being marginalised and their concerns not addressed. They were also concerned about the capacity of some institutions to absorb greater funds and whether receipt of significant support calls into question their integrity as advocates.

General Trend 4: Global Impacts

A key element of the debate on aid architecture that emerged from Asian contributions to the evaluation conference was a preoccupation with *the impotance of the global context*. Indeed, the operations of the global aid system was generally viewed by participants as an important determinant of the way aid is structured, delivered and made (or not made) effective.

One frequently identified dimension of this debate relates to the

---

37. Direct budget support – ODA channelled directly to beneficiary countries' budgets.

Northern-dominated ideological framework that 'permeates the aid system and results in the imposition of a system of knowledge and language that is coined and developed in the North' (Fernando, P, 2005:2). With specific reference to M&E systems developed by the West, some Asian contributors contended that such frameworks devalue local knowledge by bringing in externally-developed policies, tools and procedures that are little understood in recipient countries and which help to further entrench donor positions. In his contribution to the New Delhi workshop, it was argued that this type of biased ideological framework promotes knowledge production that replaces the 'blueprint *projects*' of the past with 'blueprint *approaches*' that rely on 'scientific truths and measures' – such as the Millennium Development Goals (MDGs) and poverty indicators – which depoliticise poverty reduction efforts. In so doing, a development discourse is created and institutionalised that effectively marginalises the discourse of many NGOs and social movements for change.

General Trend 5: Scepticism about aid

There is a sense of aid scepticism throughout the workshop contributions and the Asian literature on M&E and aid. These reservations are apparent in growing concerns about the influence of the post 9/11 security agenda; the question of the purposes to which aid is channelled; the common perception of 'technical assistance' as a new form of tied aid; calls for conditionality to be driven from below rather than above; in calls for greater accountability not just by recipients but also by donor countries, and finally in advocacy for reform of the international financial institutions (IFIs) and the UN system.

In contrast, the Northern debate on restructuring the international aid system has tended to deal with the system in *isolation* of its context, focussing more on technical or operational issues such as the mechanisms of aid harmonisation, developing systems of mutual accountability and designing aid conditions. So while the Northern debate is about tweaking the system's components to make it more effective, the Asian perspective was primarily about challenging the basis on which it has been conceived. This disparity of thinking flags a critical gap that needs addressing.

What Role for Asian Civil Society in ...

... Reforming the Aid System?

Changing the international aid architecture is a Northern project and it would be naïve to expect political and economic self-interest not to prevail. But at the same time, as many Southern contributors have pointed out, aid can (and often does) provide opportunities for local civil society to expand democratic space. Asian participants therefore made it clear that their participation in debates on aid reform provides a welcome opportunity to publicise their perspectives and reveal their proposals and has potential to advance the goal of strengthening Asian civil society.

There was widespread agreement at the Delhi workshop that such an inclusive strategy does not currently exist within much of Asia. It therefore emerged as a major concern that local CSOs may lose their autonomy further as they become increasingly co-opted into the aid regime as service providers to donor-supported government programmes.

Such fears did not appear to extend to the work of international NGOs, who were generally perceived as being more powerful than local CSOs in terms of their capacity to exert influence at both local and policy levels. Indeed, the impact of INGOs was also thought to be overwhelming for local CSOs. INGOs are better placed to compete for financial resources, and may undermine the growth and effectiveness of an independent, autonomous and indigenous civil society. This was vividly illustrated, participants claimed, by the international civil society response to the 2004 Asian tsunami in Asia. As expressed by both Dr. Vishaka Hidellage of ITDG Sri Lanka and Dr. Vinya Ariyaratni of Sarvodaya,[38] INGOs arrived en masse and pushed aside (even if unintentionally) local CSOs, undermining their capacity and in extreme cases leading to some of them closing down.

It is hardly surprising that workshop participants echoed calls in most studies on Asian CSOs for better capacity building of CSOs. The recent growth of CSO networks and forums is welcomed, especially those whose

---

38. ITDG or Practical Action works with community-level technology. Sarvodaya is the largest national NGO in Sri Lanka.
www.sarvodaya.org

mission statements explicitly advocate enhanced policy dialogue and information sharing. Kastuv Kanti Bandyopadhyay of PRIA noted that while well-known organisations such as BRAC have a global voice that most CSOs lack opportunities for wider exposure and are marginalised and excluded from global platforms.

... Strengthening Community Participation at National and Local Levels

In the keynote speech to the Delhi workshop, A.K. Shiva Kumar, consultant for UNICEF, pointed out that as the Government of India has become more open to involving CSOs in policy making and development planning, there was now greater scope for focus on social development issues.

Citing the recently passed Domestic Violence Bill and Right to Information Act as examples of greater CSO involvement in policy formulation, A.K. Shiva Kumar drew attention to key constraints to a stronger social development policy focus. Despite official assurances about the importance of social development, only limited resources are made available for this purpose. This is partly because the willingness of political leadership to champion social development concerns is frequently lacking. Furthermore, despite much rhetoric to the contrary, citizen participation is still not evident in many social development processes.

The keynote address drew attention to gaps in general public awareness of community development, human rights, and employment opportunities. Despite the 2005 Right to Information Act it is still difficult for the ordinary Indian citizen to access information – the Act has not turned out to be the empowering tool many hoped for. There have been insufficient efforts to influence public citizenship and build awareness of concepts of human rights, gender, and empowerment. Communities should be able to routinely access public reports and check how funds are being used. Yet, as A.K. Shiva Kumar succinctly put it; '... private grumbling about the use of resources frequently witnessed in daily life has yet to be converted into public articulation and action.'[39]

Throughout his presentation A.K. Shiva Kumar argued that local communities could not be empowered unless civil society was strengthened, for

---

[39]. For more information on A.K. Shiva Kumar's presentation at the Delhi workshop please refer to
www.intrac.org/pages/India%20papers.html

example through more regular and effective M&E of civil society participation and civic action by CSOs. He identified 'the frequent disconnect
between research/analysis and action in the programme cycle' as having
critically obstructed the ability to assess progress. He further pointed out
that because the aim of 'strengthening civil society' is a subjective concept,
one is only able to monitor progress through regular M&E processes which
predominantly focus on the overall impact of the programme, rather than
simply on inputs and outputs. Kastuv Kanti Bandyopadhyay of PRIA
echoed A.K. Shiva Kumar's call for a much greater role for M&E, i.e.' ...
monitoring and evaluation currently play a very diminutive role in the
project cycle. This is unsatisfactory'.

... Ensuring Effective Programmes Through Monitoring and Evaluation

The importance of M&E was further reiterated in a highly illuminating
keynote presentation at the Sixth Evaluation Conference ('Issues we are
Grappling With') by Sadiqa Salahuddin of Pakistan's Indus Resource Centre. Her presentation on local CSOs in Pakistan and began by highlighting
how 'appearances seem to have become more important than substance'.
Ms. Salahuddin claimed that concerns over quantity frequently eclipsed
those over quality in development programmes and highlighted the frequent failure of many CSOs to undertake adequate background research
before implementing development projects. Ms. Salahuddin claimed that
ineffectual projects were frequently allowed to continue so that 'donors
don't lose face and local CSOs keep their funding'. She accused donors of
being more interested in 'maintaining correct procedures rather than in
assessing the actual impact their interventions may be having on the
ground.'

Such statements may not come as a surprise to seasoned development
workers but they do reveal the negative implications for effective M&E
practice. As Brian Pratt later concluded; ' ... in such a context accurate, in-
depth M&E that might uncover problems and suggest changes, is unlikely
to be welcomed'.

Participatory Monitoring and Evaluation: Experiences of Asian NGOs

For a number of reasons, not least because the three selected sectors are currently very topical in Asia, the section takes a detailed look at the practice of M&E within three key areas of CSO activity – within networks or forums; advocacy and policy initiatives, and relief and rehabilitation projects.

Brief Summary of Workshop Findings

Rajesh Tandon from PRIA reflected on the disconnect between what he described as 'conventional/formal M&E methods' and 'the natural human tendency to assess.' This disparity arises, he suggested, 'because we have failed to recognise who the primary users or clients of this information actually are.' He went on to explain how formal M&E systems often stressed the importance of findings for people *other than clients* to use, and especially donors. Using M&E as tools for promoting *upward* accountability in this way however, can, he warned, result in the creation of suspicion or diminished trust between the evaluator and the organisation undertaking the evaluation. In an attempt to avoid this, participants agreed M&E activities should focus on creating approaches towards participatory learning.

More in-depth discussions on M&E practice by Asian CSOs concluded that with few exceptions M&E was generally undertaken in a top-down manner, with an emphasis on pre-determined results. Tools and techniques employed in such activities, it was argued, were those mostly imposed by donors, (e.g. logical framework analysis or LFA), and which were frequently thought to have the adverse effects of 'hampering creativity at the grassroots'. Nevertheless, there was widespread agreement among participants that field staff had found such frameworks '... to be very useful starting points'. This realisation initiated a great deal of debate amongst participants.[40] It may simply be the case that tools such as the LFA have with such frequent usage become 'institutionalised' and are now simply employed without question.

---

40. For an in-depth discussion on logical framework analysis and its alternatives, see Bakewell, O. and Garbutt, A. (2006)

There was also widespread support for the increasing use of participatory M&E (PM&E) practice. PM&E, it was noted has recently expanded to include assessment of advocacy and policy programmes, capacity building and gender mainstreaming. Whilst this expansion of remit was generally considered a good thing, participants expressed concern about the inevitable tensions between the pre-determined results generated by conventional M&E practices they employed and the unpredictable results of programmes emphasising such social development as empowerment and gender equity. Such tensions obviously demand creative resolutions, yet participants expressed doubts about the willingness and capacity of their respective organisations to do so.

In addition to the above generic participatory M&E (PME)-related findings, three key themes emerged as being especially important in Asia.

- Monitoring and evaluating the network-type organisations that are proliferating rapidly.
- Strengthening citizen monitoring of advocacy campaigns: citizen monitoring and evaluation methodologies used within the public sector require greater attention and improved documentation.
- Improved monitoring and evaluation of relief and rehabilitation programmes, including responses to the 2004 tsunami.

Monitoring & Evaluating Network Organisations

Civil society networks are now major players in global development. In the last decade, donors have placed greater emphasis on civil society voice in encouraging pro-poor development. By providing input to policy formulation processes CSOs can hold governments to account. Networks of CSOs have been the prime organisational form for articulating this voice (James & Malunga, 2006:1). Asia has witnessed a remarkable growth of networks in recent decades and networking is now generally considered to be an effective CSO activity (van der Blcek, 1999). According to Starky (1997) one reason for this proliferation has been a growing realisation among CSOs that partnering, sharing information, resources and flexibility are crucial to their long term survival (ibid:22).

Yet networks are extremely complex organisational forms to manage

effectively. They can play a multiplicity of potential and sometimes con-
flicting roles. They place considerable demands on the capacity of members
and the coordinating secretariat and are therefore far from being the simple solution sought by development planners.

With recent changes to the aid architecture, the outlook for CSO networks in Asia may be unpromising. Not only is there greater realism about
the contribution that CSO networks are able to make, but donors are beginning to question the importance of civil society as they increasingly take a
state-centred approach to development. To avoid CSO networks becoming
just another passing development fad, it is vital to understand more about
the actual contribution that CSO networks have made and to address their
inherent organisational challenges.

A case study presented in Delhi by K. Eswara Prasad of PRIA[41] attempted
to do so. Drawing on evaluation studies and change management work
undertaken with five NGO networks in Andhra Pradesh and Karnataka in
2005,[42] he argued that networks are complex systems whose effectiveness
depends on how well individual member organisations function; how well
boundaries are maintained; their ability to accommodate diverse interests
and how consistently they respond to external environments. Prasad
pointed out the important contribution of personal networking processes
– reciprocity, alliance building, conflict management, communication and
personal management – to network success. Networking, he suggested,
implies learning particular types of attitudes and behaviours: respect for
autonomy, accommodation of shared responsibility; tolerance of frequently high degrees of role ambiguity and unpredictable futures. Networks which do not take the need for such learning into account and
allocate sufficient time, opportunities and resources to acquire knowledge
and skills seem to be those which do not reach much beyond their more
task-based purposes. There is a need to respect CSOs that foster democracy,
diversity, dynamism and excellence. Prasad highlights the importance of a
'learning agenda' to keep networks evolving, but points out that such an
agenda is not embraced by many Asian networks. Some networks, it would

---

41. Prasad K.V. and Prasad A. (2005)
42. A copy of the full presentation is at
www.intrac.org/pages/PRIAWorkshop.html.
Although the study was based on only two Indian states the common threads emerging have
implications for similar efforts elsewhere.

appear, have opted to 'exist rather than to actively engage in any development schema'.

Prasad's analysis of how the complexity of network-type organisations makes it hard to assess the effectiveness and impact of their activities was further illustrated by the fact that participant discussions around identification of best impact were markedly absent at both the workshop and subsequent conference. This leads us to conclude that established evaluation mechanisms for use with Asian network organisations are still in their infancy.

This topic is creatively addressed by R. James & C. Malunga (2006:10) who write within the context of CSO networks in Malawi. Acknowledging the difficulties of directly attributing 'change' to one particular variable, such as the work of a CSO network, they nevertheless suggest that ' ... what is both possible and paramount is to be able to "plausibly associate" changes with the activities of the network'. In this regard they advise looking at the impact of CSO networks at three quite distinct levels: using representational, relationship and results indicators.

Do CSO networks represent an authentic civil society voice?

One of the biggest challenges faced by CSO networks, in Asia and elsewhere, is how to hear the views of civil society in order to be able to represent them to government. Faced with the need to react immediately to policy issues, many CSO networks simply fail to consult with their members, let alone ask them to canvass the views of their ultimate programme beneficiaries. Even when network secretariats have genuinely attempted to solicit members to share their views on certain issues they have struggled to get a clear response. Members only reply very rarely to email requests for inputs into a debate.

Whilst the difficulty of hearing from poor people via the offices of NGO members has long been acknowledged, CSO networks have been doubtful about going directly to communities themselves, for this could be interpreted as bypassing member organisations and operating independently.

Relationship Indicators; i.e. how have CSO networks related to key decision-making processes and how have these relationships been built?

At the Delhi workshop both government and CSO respondents noted that governments were initially reluctant to work with CSO networks as they were perceived as backdoor mechanisms of donor manipulation. However, over time governments appear to be understanding that CSOs have a role to play and CSO networks are increasingly viewed as government allies to help analyse issues and 'potentially even strengthen an official position albeit on a selective basis' (anonymous participant).

Over the past decade civil society engagement has become a normal and expected part of government policy development consultation processes. This is a massive shift in civil society-government relations and one that can undoubtedly be ascribed to the work of CSO networks (James and Chirwa 2002). Many Asian governments now actively solicit the views of civil society and invite CSO networks to be part of key decision-making fora as a matter of course.

The elusive indications of CSO networking results

As James & Malunga (2006) point out, 'all this representation and relationship makes little difference unless the content and implementation of policies have changed' (ibid:15). So what impact has the work of CSO networks really had on poverty reduction in Asia?

As many CSO networks are still young and because poverty is so deeply entrenched, Asian participants felt that this was a difficult question to answer. They did point out however that the work of some of the more prominent CSO networks has enabled civil society to have an input into policy formulation processes to a degree not accomplished before.

Chirwa and Nyirenda (2002) discuss how the contribution of networks to poverty reduction can be effectively viewed at two different levels: a change in welfare or a change in the policy environment and service delivery mechanisms that ultimately influence the change in welfare. Asian networks, like others, have had a more direct influence on the policy environment but have tended to measure only their activities – the government policies they have influenced – rather than the results of this in terms of poverty alleviation. It is therefore difficult to assess the difference that Asian CSO networks have made to poverty reduction. It is only possible to note a number of actual and potential contributions.

Monitoring and Evaluating Policy Dialogue and Advocacy

As policy and advocacy campaigns have grown exponentially it is imperative that we seek answers to fundamental questions: What are the current practices for evaluating the effects and impacts of policy dialogue and advocacy? What methods, approaches and tools are appropriate to such evaluation practices? What lessons can be drawn? These were questions posed by conference facilitators at both the Delhi workshop and the sixth evaluation conference. The following case studies show some useful real-life examples.

Mahbubul Karim of PROSHIKA, a leading Bangladesh NGO founded the Institute for Development Policy Analysis and Advocacy (IDPAA), evaluated a campaign started in 1994 to make the national budget a participatory and pro-poor tool to tackle mass poverty. The campaign, which has had a significant impact on Bangladesh's budget-making process, has challenged elite bias in Bangladeshi governance and the non-participatory and bureaucratic control of budget-making. Budgets are growth-centered with little consideration of poverty-eradication. The IDPAA campaign has been systematically advocating policy measures to secure equity alongside growth. Even small successes need to be recognised and celebrated, a belief underpinning the 'appreciative enquiry' type methodology employed to evaluate the campaign. The two key questions posed by IDPAA and partners at each stage of the campaign, and as each minor victory has been identified, have been: what has changed in the short term and what has changed in the long term? Most donor reviews of PROSHIKA programmes in 1997–2000 applauded both the budget campaign and the evaluation mechanisms. IDPAA has since adopted the success-based approach to assess and evaluate all its advocacy activities.

Yogesh Kumar of the Indian NGO Samarthan described how staff have selected a conventional M&E methodology to evaluate advocacy campaigns. Samarthan has developed a clear and flexible action plan and follow-up strategy using structured formats of questionnaires for systematic monitoring. Monitoring has been supported through a core group of involved people and regular feedback mechanisms. Some of the more difficult aspects of the monitoring process have included:

- use of qualitative indicators for assessing outcomes and impacts
- the need to accommodate multiple actors at multiple levels
- remembering the importance of collective accountability when reporting findings
- setting overly ambitious targets and policy-influencing agendas
- initial failure to negotiate local power dynamics.

Puranjeet Banerjee analysed the evaluation methodology employed by PRIA in its policy and advocacy campaigns. Selecting the right policy priorities and regular analysis of the changing circumstances of an advocacy campaign is essential. Mobilisation of civil society groups and support from the media has underpinned success of two key campaigns in the Indian state of Madhya Pradesh – the Pre-Election Voters' Awareness Campaign (PEVAC) for local elections and the *'Wada-Na-Todo Abhiyan'* ('Keep Your Promise Campaign'). PRIA has recognised the need to:

- define the process in its particular context before developing an appropriate evaluation method for its assessment
- develop clear but flexible action plans and follow-up processes
- ensure targets are attainable: overly ambitious targets are difficult to assess and can result in raising the expectations of campaign participants
- create regular feedback mechanisms: a web-based mechanism for Wada-Na-Todo Abhiyan and simple bottom-up feedback mechanisms for PEVAC have been effective
- undertake joint stakeholder assessments and an in-house review of events on completion of each major step of a campaign
- acknowledge that advocacy type campaigns are processes without finite dates and parameters: assessing impact is therefore far from straightforward!
- realise that linear cause and effect relationships used in methodologies based logical framework approaches are highly inappropriate for evaluating policy dialogue and advocacy: however, unstructured log-frame matrices can be used.

- appreciate that indicators of outcomes and impact are frequently unpredictable
- strengthening the capacity of civil society to participate in both the campaign and its assessment
- remember to celebrate even small successes as the stepping-stone for larger successes.

Anju Dwivedi of PRIA made an extensive presentation on strengthening citizen monitoring – a fashionable methodology identified by participants as constituting the most effective means of strengthening local participation, accountability and transparency within governance institutions. Citizen monitoring, he described, is a process of including citizens in checking, observing, collecting information on development plans, policies and programmes. It is about taking action on the gaps that might exist for achieving desired outcomes by holding the higher authorities of state, bilateral and multilateral agencies accountable in order to help promote effective and robust governance. Citizen monitoring is a process which focuses on people's rights to ascertain that their interests are not compromised while also ensuring that in protecting their interests people do not jettison the larger 'public good'. It is a method that enables participants to

Local Government

exercise their rights and examine the nature of their civic duties. It is a way to measure the real outcomes of projects, programmes or schemes. The visible results that the process yields tend to address the *real* issues, and the demonstrable impacts of the programme are useful instruments for citizen-led advocacy.

Anju Dwivedi pointed out that in India at least, the concept of citizen monitoring has yet to be officially accepted. In his view this is primarily because the term 'monitoring' has traditionally been associated with a body of skills which only development 'experts' were believed to possess. There is an impression that M&E is such a specialised and technical area that 'community' is not experienced enough to handle monitoring on their own. Such a narrow view of monitoring has stifled people's active contribution in solving their own problems. It is important, he argued, to demystify monitoring if people's participation in projects and programmes is to be ensured.

Participants were also equally aware of the drawbacks of this approach, however, and in small group discussions made these comments:

> 'There is an obvious disconnect between the results produced by citizen monitoring and the nature of the log-frames that the results feed into.'

> 'Citizen monitoring can be costly (financially and otherwise) for the citizens participating in the process.'

> 'It is difficult to consolidate or document learning from such large-scale processes.'

> 'The donor employing this approach has to be impartial, so as not to alienate the community.'

Yet such awareness appeared to have done little to put most participants off this methodology. Indeed, such drawbacks were simply put down to the fact that citizens monitoring was still 'an evolving art form within the continent'.

PRIA has amassed a wealth of experience in the use of citizensí monitoring. It has worked in partnership with local NGOs in India and Sri Lanka. Anju Dwivedi identified the key steps underlining its approach:

- identification of key issue and problems
- identification of interested actors and their roles
- developing indicators and action plans
- collection and analysis of information
- taking action at the lowest level and demanding action from the higher authorities.

PRIA experience has taught it that the term 'monitoring' can have negative connotations. As it evokes fear and resentment a non-threatening environment needs to be built to get the support of all stakeholders. Monitoring provides opportunity for citizen action and space for people to take responsibility for their own lives. While ensuring accountability from higher authorities is essential, it is also important that citizens demonstrate responsibility to the state and other institutions. In this way, citizenship processes can be strengthened in the community.

PRIA has noted that low citizen participation and failure to provide communities with information weakens accountability. Although projects often aim to ensure community participation from the planning stage, in practice communities are only required to acquiesce on pre-conceptualised and pre-designed projects.

Multiparty accountability can be established through citizen monitoring: In any community there may be a variety of institutions present which function independently of each other. Through citizen monitoring, a process of mutual accountability can be established amongst those different institutions.

Experience shows that citizen monitoring can be empowering for the voiceless and marginalised. It provides opportunities for them to explain things as they see them and to analyse, plan and carry through a course of planned action. This is made possible when they are equipped with the analytical and action-oriented skills necessary for them to become actively involved in development.

Dwivedi concluded by noting key obstacles to citizen monitoring.

Rigid Administrative Structures: In locations where the political environment does not encourage openness or citizens' voices, decision-making is controlled and administrative structures deny space for participation it is unlikely that people would raise their voices to demand their rights and responses from high-level officials. Persistent non-responsiveness can disillusion citizens further.

*Social Dilemmas:*The disempowered do not constitute a homogeneous group. Subsequently the problems faced by them are often varied and very different from those who are more advantaged. The process of facilitating people to be empowered to demand their rights is fraught with resistance from more advantaged and powerful groups.

Citizens' monitoring is a very powerful process. To date the meaning of participation has been very narrowly understood and its relation with accountability has remained blurred. It is important that citizen monitoring as a process is integrated in all types of programmes so that accountability and transparency are established between citizens and statutory/non-statutory institutions right from the start.

Better monitoring practices from the design of projects can lead to better ownership of projects even when outside implementing agencies e.g. donors withdraw. Monitoring should be viewed as process that gives the disempowered the space to voice their concerns, develop strategies for taking action and demand responsiveness from higher level institutions.

Democratic decentralisation offers tremendous opportunities for the promotion of citizens monitoring as this policy favours grassroots democracy and power is being gradually bestowed on village level institutions. This methodology can promote effective governance through the establishment of better accountability mechanisms and greater responsiveness of higher level institutions.

Such was the interest generated by the topic of citizen monitoring in the Delhi workshop that conference organisers felt it would be beneficial for further, more in-depth discussions. Participants were thus divided into two small groups and requested to reflect on:

- how citizen monitoring and evaluation can enable civic engagement and interface between governance institutions and citizens
- the methods, approaches, tools, and techniques which enable citizen monitoring and evaluation
- how it can be mainstreamed in policies, institutions and programmes

- the challenges and opportunities for promoting citizen monitoring and evaluation.

Participants noted that citizens' monitoring is not only about the monitoring of CSO projects but can also be effectively employed in monitoring government service delivery mechanisms. This would strengthen citizen participation and confidence levels and make governance institutions more accountable. In this way bottom-up monitoring processes can help bring about change at the top.

Another participant explained how the decentralisation process in India currently facilitated programme implementation at central, state and local levels but stressed that it is the government's role to outsource the delivery of specific public services to NGOs. Consequently, citizen monitoring was very important in enabling citizens to oversee the proper utilisation of funds. Encouragingly, the role of CSOs in bottom-up planning is rapidly expanding in line with the increased participation of grassroots representatives.

Abhijit Sen, a member of The Planning Commission of India, pointed out that the Government of India has launched many poverty eradication programmes involving livelihood and income-generation initiatives. The speaker claimed that such programmes needed to be carefully evaluated before generalisations could be made about their success or otherwise. Sen emphasised the importance of employing *process-related evaluation tech- niques* in place of the more frequently employed task-oriented evaluations in order to assess effectiveness. Sen discussed the possibility of establishing and utilising standard assessment methods/frameworks in all the states of India. Although he acknowledged the difficulty of employing one-size-fits-all methods he believed that the process of 'setting up ombudsmen' or a 'complaint centre at Panchayat[43] level' would encourage citizens to come forward and provide feedback on what does and does not work. In order to do this, however, he conceded that the accounting capacity of Panchayati Raj institutions would need to be built up first to accommodate such findings. Sen pointed out that the planning process undertaken by the Planning Commission could provide the space needed for citizen monitoring to be employed more routinely.

Participants agreed that the enormous amount of learning derived from

---

43. Panchayati Raj – an administrative unit (panchayat) of five villages.

this methodology would be difficult to compile or document. In order to make such initiatives more widely acceptable, they suggested that Northern practitioners should aim to sensitise donors to the relevance of this tool, especially its potential interface with flexible log-frames.

Monitoring & Evaluating Disaster Relief & Rehabilitation Programmes

Devastation caused by the 2004 Asian tsunami and the 2006 Pakistan earthquake again highlighted the importance of developing effective M&E approaches for use in disaster relief and rehabilitation programmes. Key speakers related experiences of undertaking such M&E.

Padma Glacilda Ratnayake, of Sri Lanka's South Asia Partnership described challenges faced by her agency and other CSOs when attempting to evaluate relief and rehabilitation programmes in the immediate aftermath of the tsunami. She recited an all-too-familiar catalogue of errors:

- lack of co-ordination among and between NGOs and government
- difficulties in auditing the overall cost of relief and rehabilitation work
- insufficient capacity of some NGOs to undertake relief and rehabilitation work
- inability of under-equipped NGOs to say 'no' to work they were unable to undertake
- absence of any type of M&E of effort or impact studies
- failure to prepare a coordination database
- absence of effective relief and rehabilitation policies
- failure to introduce a 'framework' for M&E activities, thus leading to lack of efforts to build the credibility of local NGOs.

The wider debate that ensued following this presentation in the Netherlands highlighted the significant challenges faced in all tsunami-affected Asian countries. Shortcomings of the post-tsunami approach to rehabilitation indicate the need to:

- monitor corruption and malpractice in such chaotic situations
- assist local NGOs to evaluate their own programmes in the wider context of other organisations and government policy

- allow NGOs to occasionally play the role of service providers in place of government, and focus more on longer-term development than on disaster management and preparedness.
- help NGOs to develop context-specific indicators and mechanisms for assessing disaster relief and rehabilitation
- ensure local community members are involved in development of evaluatory mechanisms.

This last point proved controversial and led some conference participants to voice their scepticism about community involvement in disaster management. However, Ms. Ratnayake assured participants that every effort would be made to build the capacity of disaster mitigation teams in villages through mock drills and the preparation of disaster action plans. Participatory methods such as social and resource mapping were being adopted so as to strengthen community involvement in disaster mitigation plans. She reiterated the need for more advocacy work with governments so that disaster management is not perceived as an isolated/separate entity, but as part and parcel of longer-term development programmes.

Current CSO M&E Dilemmas in Humanitarian Crises

Arguably the most prevalent dilemma currently facing Asian CSOs working on disaster management issues relates to the choice they have to make about whether to scale-up/expand (thereby increasing their absorption capacity and ability to handle such crises) or to simply change focus by improving their advocacy strategies on such key rights-based issues as land rights and gender equality.

Another less explicit dilemma relates to the emerging need for CSOs to be able to accurately monitor the use of funds donated for disaster relief. This is an area in which the development of effective M&E mechanisms could have a potentially significant impact. Unfortunately, such mechanisms seem markedly absent. Participants highlight a number of reasons for this. The first relates to the notable disconnect between M&E systems employed during peace-time and those deployed for relief operations. As one participant succinctly put it; 'M&E is rarely a priority in peace-time, so therefore can't be expected to take priority in times of crisis'.

A second reason relates to the insufficient levels of learning from assessments of previous disaster experience. Contributing to this gap are the difficulties of effective time-management when undertaking M&E of emergency interventions and the high rate of staff turn-over. Hugh Goyder identified a specific phenomenon known as *'the retreat syndrome'* which he described as being the gradual loss of experienced staff members as emergency situations move beyond crisis point, and the related loss of institutional memory that results. To make matters worse, there is frequently reliance on *'the technical fix phenomena'* - the belief that disasters can be 'fixed' through almost purely technological interventions. This partiality for technocratic solutions is also evidenced by the kind of staff recruited for emergencies as INGOs prefer those with technical, rather than social, development expertise.

Each disaster is different from others, a further factor having a significant impact on the manner in which disasters are managed and assessed. The shortage of CSOs and INGOs in Kashmir, and the highly conservative nature of governments in other Asian countries, are thought to have severely hampered attempts to manage emergencies (Salahuddin, 2006).

Emergencies such as the 2006 earthquake in Pakistan have had both positive and negative impacts on local CSOs. The disaster has become the focus of many new emergency strategies implemented by COS but on the other hand there has been rushed scaling-up of agencies with inadequate planning of changes to their structure or systems. The all-too-common post-disaster problem of INGOs poaching CSO staff has weakened local organisations and drastically altered organisational cultures and expectations.

Role of the Media in a Humanitarian Crisis

Conference organisers thought it important for participants to be able to discuss this hitherto ignored subject in the aftermath of the tsunami and Pakistani earthquake. We were fortunate enough to have journalists in our midst during the evaluation conference and therefore able to attain an 'insider's view'.

Despite widespread agreement that the initial role of the media during a humanitarian crisis is to provide information, participants involved in relief and rehabilitation (R&R) work also made mention of the more 'adversarial role' taken by the media as the scale of disasters gradually unfolds.

Two participants in particular expressed frustration at the fact that journalists would often compete with their organisations to inform the world of major catastrophes. Always appearing to be one step ahead, journalists were accused of frequently oversimplify complex issues underlying crises. This led a small group of conference participants to question what mechanisms could be employed to harness the media's support to the relief and development goals of CSOs.

Aliya Salahuddin, a Pakistani journalist, unravelled the complex linkages and interfaces between the role of the media (both local and international) and the needs of relief and development CSOs in the aftermath of the Pakistan earthquake. She showed that obstacles to aid agencies are also obstacles to media – the size of the devastated area, rugged and mountainous terrain, landslides, bad weather breakdown of basic services and collapse of communications made it hard for aid agencies and the media to collaborate.

The dilemmas and questions that arise out of evaluation concerns can be turned into issues of open debate once the media gets involved. It is good to have media discussion of debates around prioritising relief work and reconstruction, where resources should be allocated and whether progress can be measured by restoring infrastructure or by making qualitative improvements. Media engagement in such brainstorming allows everyone involved in the relief and reconstruction process to understand the issues. The media can help aid CSOs communicate their concerns and suggestions to governments, donors and each other. The media can play a potent advocacy role helping to sell CSO recommendations to local and national government structures.

Salahuddin noted that poverty always exacerbates the outcome of any disaster. It is known, for example, that it wasn't simply the earthquake that killed people, but that poor infrastructure and faulty construction were responsible for most deaths, victims' poor living conditions and lack of medical aid. With media support aid agencies can highlight the needs of vulnerable populations and areas before a disaster actually takes place. Poverty may then become a more serious media issue than it currently is.

In Pakistan's current political circumstances, the media can play only a limited role in data gathering and analysis. For the media to be used as a means of evaluating aid response, vital changes are needed to enable aid agencies, CSOs and the media must be able to work together for promotion of democracy, building and strengthening democratic institutions and publicising information, including results of internal monitoring. There must be freedom to access sources of information and freedom to dissent from state-controlled established opinions.

If the media industry are to be humanitarian partners, aid agencies must provide them with research data, human interest stories, access to communities they work with and a factual, readily understood assessment of needs, successes and failures. Media linkages can help civil society transform an image which has been tainted in Pakistan by conspiracy theorists who see a malevolent Western agenda behind any internationally supported innovation.

The Pakistani media, as in other developing countries, is strapped for resources. Donors should consider providing scholarships in journalism and enabling exchange programmes to help media workers techniques of documentary making

Ms Salahuddin also noted potential for CSOs to work with the media to work together to:

- tackle gender stereotyping.
- encourage the government to take a new approach to media management and allow the media to assess the transparency of government activities
- allow the media to empower the powerless with information, ideas and opinions and to unleash its potential to be a social reformer. an educator, a pressure group and a platform for encouraging debate in a country where democratic institutions do not exist
- empower people to ask the right questions during a massive movement of people, resources and money.

It is vital to acknowledge that the community and the affected must be allowed to speak for themselves. There is a great danger that the media and CSOs claim to speak on their behalf or about them but without listening to their voices or allowing them even to be heard.

CSOs and the media must jointly push for a national disaster preparedness plan for Pakistan. Building a more trusting and constructive relationship with one another is the only way to forge more productive, accountable and transparent partnerships.

Summary of Findings and Concluding Comments

The Asian workshop focused on monitoring and evaluating topics that sit on the margins between development, community and politics. Empowerment, citizenship, activism, free media and advocacy were all important topics.

As we noted at the beginning of the chapter there is much scepticism in Asia about post 9/11 changes to the aid disbursement system and new enthusiasms for technical assistance and tied aid. But what is the role for Asian CSOs in reforming the aid system?

Aid provides an instrument that local CSOs can use to strive for expanded democratic space. As Southern participants pointed out time and again, there are very few international fora where Southern CSOs can articulate their views about the current functioning of the international aid system, and where they can discuss proposals for reform.

However, CSOs will be unable to play a significant role in contributing to the aid reform process unless they invest sufficient resources in building their capacity. The testimonies in this chapter have shown that Asian CSOs have a critical function in strengthening community participation in decision-making, even at national levels. The major obstacle to this happening more frequently is the notable disconnect between research and analysis and the implementation of CSO programmes designed to strengthen participation. It is obvious that M&E needs to play a far greater role in CSO programmes than it does currently. Donors could further support this process by focussing more on 'substance than appearance' and enabling the M&E which is undertaken to uncover existing problems and suggest changes for improvement.

The scope of M&E practice in Asia is also rapidly expanding to encompass relatively new CSO functions such as networking, advocacy and policy activities. However, this expansion in scope has highlighted existing tensions between the pre-determined results generated by conventional M&E and the unpredictable results of social development programmes. Such tensions require a creativity and transformation of the donor-CSO relationships, which is not yet apparent.

M&E of CSO Network Organisations

There has been a great proliferation of CSO network organisations in Asia within recent years. However, these types of organisations have had difficulty in developing and utilising effective M&E frameworks with which to 'prove' their effectiveness and contribution to poverty alleviation agendas. Current changes in the global aid system especially the increasingly state-centred emphasis, makes it imperative to demonstrate such proof. Without it, network organisations may not survive in the long-term. A greater respect for 'learning' and the introduction of effective learning agendas are, all participants agreed the ways forward. An M&E framework that comprise the assessment of 'representational', 'relationship' and 'results' indicators provides an example of more appropriate frameworks for use by CSO networks.

M&E of Advocacy and Policy Programmes

Asian advocacy organisations have faced difficulties in developing appropriate M&E frameworks for strengthening their activities. The linear cause and effect relationships involved in M&E methodologies based on the popular LFA have been found to be highly inappropriate for these types of organisations. Methods that are currently being employed (quite successfully) in assessing advocacy programmes include the 'appreciative enquiry' methodology; use of 'unstructured LFA methods' and most popularly the 'citizens' monitoring' methodology. The latter is widely applauded by many Asian CSOs as it is believed to be a unique bottom-up monitoring process that can be utilised to bring about change at the top. In India and elsewhere in Asia this methodology is yet to be officially recognised, partly because it is considered to be 'too threatening' to government and because the term 'monitoring' is still wrongly associated with 'technical expertise and skills' that communities are 'unable to master'.

M&E of Disaster Relief and Rehabilitation

Participants noted that one of the many challenges faced by CSOs working in disaster situations is the absence of suitable M&E frameworks for assessing their efforts and impacts. A notable failing in existing M&E systems has been the lack of local participation in ascertaining the quality of changes that may have occurred as a result of these programmes. Although there have been calls (mostly by donors) for greater community involvement in the development and use of suitable M&E systems, there has also been a real resistance to this by those higher up the government hierarchy and even by some local CSOs. The general belief still persists that M&E is a specialised set of techniques which community groups are unable to grasp. This situation has to change if M&E findings and CSO functions are ever to gain the legitimacy and credibility they desperately seek.

4

Central Asia, the Caucasus and Eastern Europe: From Statist to Activist

Esther Mebrahtu and Linda Lönnqvist

The Former Soviet Union (FSU) is a region that has seen one of the most dramatic structural turnarounds in recent times – from interdependent units in a complex and all-encompassing central planning system, to independence as autonomous states, with all the risks and freedoms that entails. The state/civil society dichotomy is therefore relatively new and civil society organisations (CSOs) are only now forging their own space. The legacy of five-year plans and years of dependence on a massive level of quantitative feedback shapes the work of CS M&E. Enormous changes to established paradigms and ways of thinking will be required in order to adapt to small-scale, process-oriented M&E.

Most of the examples and experiences in this chapter come from Central Asia. Eastern European, Balkan and Caucasian views are also discussed since they arose at the geographical discussion group at the sixth evaluation conference. Hence, the chapter begins with an overview of the Central Asian background.

Introduction: A Short Analysis of the Development of Civil Society in the Former Soviet Union[44]

With the break up of the Soviet Union in 1991, independence was, essentially, thrust upon the Central Asian republics. They were suddenly faced with the task of building nation states and market economies in new countries previously structured around specialised production for the unitary Soviet state. As in other parts of the FSU this sudden politico-economic change initially led to a slump in production and to a general slide into acute poverty (Earle et al, 2005).[45]

Subsequent economic and political developments, variable pace of policy reform and unequal access to natural resources have given rise to marked differences in growth, stability, economic independence and social development across Central Asia, the Caucasus and Eastern Europe.

A Brief History of Civil Society in Central Asia

Central Asia has a long history of 'communal civil society'. For centuries both nomadic and settled agricultural communities had mutual savings schemes and other traditional collective endeavours (Moldesheva & Buxton, 2006:2). The Soviet period then saw the development of public associations of a completely different type, reflecting the socialist state's rapid modernisation strategy and one-party political system. Such associations included scientific, cultural and political organisations and all kinds of interest groups and committees reaching down to village levels. It was not until Mikhail Gorbachev introduced perestroika in the mid 1980s that contemporary civil society was born in Central Asia.

Moldesheva and Buxton (2006) identify three defining characteristics of Central Asian civil society:

• a notable urban-rural divide: the more robust local NGOs are located in the capital cities and provincial centres

---

44. This chapter draws on Moldosheva A. and Buxton, C. (2006), *Internal report for Oxfam-Novib Research Project, Central Asia and Global Civil Society*, INTRAC.

45. Earle L. et al. (2005). *The Development of Civil Society in Central Asia*, INTRAC.

- the marked role of female leaders: women are commonly found in key leadership positions in civil society organisations (CSOs)
- a notable willingness on the part of local NGOs to work alongside government and dependence on the state to ultimately take responsibility for addressing all social development needs.

Local NGO Strengths and Weaknesses

The newness and relative smallness of civil society, together with the socio-economic crises of the transition period, have greatly limited the ability of Central Asia CSOs to frame and achieve their own agendas. Many were established by dominant and charismatic individuals (usually one of the founders) frequently without a clear comprehension of niche or mission. Many lack significant financial and non-financial resources and often have underdeveloped management structures. However, within the core of the most active and professionally run NGOs, there is significant technical and management expertise. Many have well-educated and experienced staff and increasingly CSOs are recognising the need to improve internal governance.

The majority of NGOs in Central Asia are still dependent on external donors. This is particularly true in aid-dependent Kyrgyzstan and Tajikistan. Government funding to NGOs is still in its infancy. The short-term nature of much international funding, together with dependence on government funding secured through tenders and contracts, limits CSOs' capacity for organisational development.

Issues that Emerged from the Sixth International Conference

It was strikingly apparent during the evaluation conference that Central Asia differs markedly from many of the underdeveloped regions in which INGOs have traditionally worked. Central Asia is made up of newly-fledged 'second world' countries whose key commonality is their recent history as Soviet republics. They are also characterised by the dominant role played by state institutions, economic downturn and chequered progress towards parliamentary democracy.

Significantly, Central Asian and other FSU states do not view themselves as 'developing countries' in the traditional sense of the term. Regional conference participants stressed that they find such a label to be demeaning. The turmoil of post-communist transition and inappropriate policy responses have created a complex situation in which poverty and inequality have grown apace. However, Central Asians do not identify with the world's least developed states. During the Soviet era the literacy rate reached 95%. Social support systems generally worked effectively, undoubtedly providing welfare and development gains to the general population, and leaving the region with a legacy of strong viable state structures.

The peoples of Central Asia are well aware that the region has to adapt in order to prosper in a changing world. Local civil society is now looking to the future. As one participant noted:

> 'There was a time when people in Central Asia blotted out the past. Now that attitude is changing and people are beginning to look critically at the past and trying to identify what was good and bad about it.'

Ongoing Power of Technocratic States

Former Soviet states have always had, and continue to have, a very dominant quantitative/technocratic tradition which is generally accepted. This is not necessarily a bad thing for the technocratic approach has been considered quite effective in attaining centrally-planned goals. However, participants alluded to the fact that government remains essentially unaccountable. There is little sense that the state should be open to scrutiny – there is certainly no culture of evaluation of state bodies in the region.

It follows therefore that there are limited numbers of evaluators in the region and evaluation is predominantly viewed as a procedure associated with local NGOs and CSOs. In Central Asia, as in the rest of the FSU, state officials still rely on official statistics for information from the ground. However, there are positive indications that governments are beginning to be exposed to, and recognise the value of, client-based participatory approaches such as Poverty Monitoring methodologies.[46]

---

46. INTRAC has had an important role in introducing PRA to NGOs and communities in Kyrgyzstan.

These can help to ensure people feel they have more power over their lives but participants pointed out that they can also be very time-consuming and intensive.

In the post-Soviet era there was much initial resistance to participatory methods. Qualitative approaches, and PRA in particular, were viewed as being both unscientific and even humiliating. However, those who have adopted participatory M&E methods are currently seeing there benefits (even as far up as the national level) and accumulating experience of positive case studies. Two examples were provided from Kyrgyzstan of the Ministries of Health and Labour which have seen the benefits of participatory approaches and now want to adopt some of these methods. 'The changes in peoples' behaviour is tangible and visible', noted a Kyrgyz official.

Despite these recent trends however, regional governments remain very focused on their role as service providers. A number of conference participants flagged the need for thorough rethinking of the state's role, for currently there is only very limited space for civil society in service provision. Many regional governments have very large departments who are the main executors and implementers of social projects. Consequently, there are few channels through which civil society could engage with government on any of these issues. There is no real participation from the community in how these bureaucracies undertaken research and planning and as a result little has been done to promote M&E practices. The dominant feeling in the region seems to be that the government is a monolith that doesn't effectively interface with civil society. There are two closed systems and never the twain shall meet!

It is critically important to ask how things can change, to explore ways in which government and civil society might interact in a more effective and mutually beneficial manner. Some participants believed the only solution to be major and unwieldy administrative reform. They explained that in the few instances where CSOs did engage with state structures, they were always defensive, on the back foot, too small to stand up for their own interests and beliefs. Finding it hard to negotiate, they often end up having to cut financial corners to survive. There is thus a need for training and awareness-raising of the importance of collaboration between the public and NGO sectors.

Despite the general lack of engagement, there are encouraging instances of cooperation. The Kazakh government, for example, provides substantial support for civil society social development programmes. It has links with NGOs – although these are usually established on the basis of personal connections, frequently because the wife of a bureaucrat works for an NGO. Clearly this can results in risks of nepotism or corruption, but it is encouraging that the government is enabling local NGOs to run social projects and act as service providers.[47]

From Albania, we heard examples of widespread CS-local government cooperation on certain undertakings e.g. surveys/census, the results of which are then offered to national government through mutually supportive processes. On the other hand, Bosnian participants at the conference reported an ongoing obsession with quantitative data at the level of government. They explained that at this level, quantitative monitoring (although not evaluation!) methods such as the use of statistics were common, and even suggested that unless monitoring data was statistical in nature; the results would not be taken seriously. However, they did also warn that there is a need to 'move away from the traditional language and approaches to monitoring' if this trend is ever to be reversed and qualitative information included. Later, one to one discussions revealed that there are examples of qualitative evaluation initiatives being undertaken at community level, although in many cases the results of such exercises are not officially recognised at higher levels.

Participatory approaches are working but are still weak ...

Participatory methods have been received with mixed reviews in Central Asia. On the one hand, those who have worked with them recognise their value and endeavour to incorporate them within their operating structures. However, many are reluctant to use them, in part to the fact that participatory methods were introduced to the region without sufficient regard for local context. Participants spoke of feeling extremely patronised by foreign PRA practitioners talking about learning from 'bean counting in an African village' and stressing the value of diagrams over verbal communication. They continually emphasised the importance of locally appropriate adaptation of tools and methodologies. As one Kazakh participant put it: '... the

---

47. Ministry officials contend that the system is kept deliberately 'closed' to local NGOs, primarily in order to better control the situation.

great idea of PRA is to communicate. [It demonstrates] how people can think through and plan techniques. It is important to note that we did not use the tools as given, such as using beans for counting, but developed our own culturally appropriate tools.'

Many participants were interested in adapting tools for local use and spreading the participatory ethos. As one Kazakh participant noted:

> 'It [is important] to have an understanding of how to use and approach PRA. It is about changing our thinking and not just adopting a toolbox! We need to think differently – move from "top down approaches". It is very difficult to talk about roles and behaviours. People are more interested in outputs.'

The question of whether participatory approaches in general, and participatory M&E in particular, are accepted and actually working in Central Asia cannot be definitively answered at this stage. Such approaches have not evolved from this culture and will time to be assimilated. However, early indications are positive. A small number of CSOs are striving to find ways around mechanisms or processes that are not readily transferable to the local context and to overcome historical legacies. As M&E feedback sessions are not always seen as appropriate – and may be reminiscent of Soviet era public highlighting of mistakes – they are finding ways to commend staff on positive steps they take. As one participant remarked:

> 'One of the problems with M&E is that we often forget basic psychology – the importance of giving praise rather than criticism of progress.'

M&E Language: Too much Jargon!

Echoing complaints frequently made at every M&E conference/workshop, Central Asian participants noted the opaque and unhelpful nature of M&E-related terminology. HelpAge Moldova complained that 'the jargon of M&E seems to be a real barrier to our work' and how alien terms distract attention away from core issues that need to be addressed. HelpAge Moldova has taken a different approach, working directly with communities and asking questions without using the standard language of monitoring. They especially avoided getting 'hung up' on terminology.

Oxfam is working in the Caucasus and Albania where its work is progressing effectively. As with the situation in Moldova, terminology – not language – was believed to be the main barrier.

Can the term 'development' be used in Central Asia?

In a hotly contested debate on the theme of 'development' in Central Asia, the question was raised whether Central Asians should abandon the term or take a different approach. There was a strong sense that experiences from the FSU (and south-eastern Europe) could enrich thinking about development as a whole and contribute to debates. Their perspective is one of belonging to Second and not Third World countries. They feel that the Second World should be encouraged by donors and global institutions to find its own way of enriching other debates and contexts. This feeling was reflected in an earlier discussion on language and jargon.

Conclusion

The FSU can bring a different and valuable angle to our basic understanding of 'development', especially since there are such a variety of countries with different experiences in the region. Central Asian and Eastern European participants at the sixth evaluation conference started to break new ground by reworking M&E language to their own needs, and rejecting international jargon which didn't fit their situation.

To sum up, the key points that emerged from the Central Asia session were:

1. concern about the way donors are tempted to focus on democratisation in FSU, as opposed to basic needs

2. a belief that while donor support to governments (e.g. via aid harmonisation) is understandable, this should not detract from the need to focus on the vital need to build a strong well-networked civil society in the region

3. a strong feeling that the term 'development' should either be expanded to encapsulate the situation in the region or dropped

4. recognition that while participatory approaches have been introduced to the region they have yet to gain a foot-hold in routine behaviour and practice: there is still an emphasis on need for more tools rather than for changing attitudes!

5. conviction that standard M&E jargon is obtrusive and needs to be dropped or modified to fit the local context

6. concern that there is still an emphasis on 'accountancy' rather than 'accountability'

7. awareness that analytical capacity is severely underdeveloped: there is a lack of real understanding of context and changes to the context

8. recognition of lack of space for civil society and lack of political will to create it

9. stress on the importance of recognising the diversity in Central Asia as well as the diversity of donor's agendas.

5

Latin America

Esther Mebrahtu and Brian Pratt

Introduction: Rethinking International Cooperation from a Latin American Perspective

Latin America is a very heterogeneous continent, with a rich history, not least in the field of pioneering development thinking. It is thus difficult to make generalisations about how current changes in the aid architecture have impacted on this area, and the type of aid strategies that have been used. Although it is widely accepted that aid levels are significant within the poorest countries in the continent, the focus on trade is much more prevalent in the higher-income countries. Moreover, in many instances aid to Latin America has been closely linked to the struggle against drugs as well as to other geo-political and commercial interests.

Official Development Assistance (ODA) to Latin America has declined significantly since 1994. For many donors, the UK and the EU in particular, Latin America is simply not a priority. Many donors have reoriented their aid to a small number of less-developed countries with which they have long-standing historical ties. Indeed, Spain remains by far the largest donor to the region. Direct foreign investment surpasses aid in the more economically advanced areas of the continent, although countries like Bolivia, Haiti, Honduras and Nicaragua remain very heavily aid-dependent. Remittances from migrant workers have started to surpass aid volumes for many of these countries.

A review of the Latin American literature by academics from this region highlights a certain degree of antipathy over the fact that most proposals for reforms in the aid system have, to date, come from North America and Europe. This is put down to the excess of resources in the North, i.e. 'Northern organisations are the ones who have the means to promote research, discussion, and diffusion on these issues' according to one workshop participant. A great deal of resentment exists over the fact that most global aid policy debates are held in the English language and that there is minimal acknowledgement of Latin American contributions. Separation between Anglophone and Hispanic development activities is largely caused by the language difference.

International Assistance and Inequality

Discussions held at the Sixth Evaluation Conference indicated many Latin Americans don't subscribe totally to the Paris Declaration idea of a new paradigm of 'aid effectiveness' founded on a discourse of country-led partnership and co-responsibility. Donors have become more selective in targeting only low-income countries in Latin America for poverty alleviation, but throughout the continent poverty and inequality levels continue to remain very high even in the middle income countries. Participants therefore questioned how aid to Latin America could help reduce inequality given the fact that the state has so far failed to do so. Although the continent has seen a range of very different regimes through modern historical times, inequality still remains stubbornly persistent. It was generally felt that donors should focus on finding a balance between direct and indirect poverty alleviation strategies to help at least middle-income countries in the region to meet the MDGs.

Latin American participants did not feel that the newly celebrated issue of 'country ownership' could be discussed within the context of the Paris Declaration, as there was thought to be a glaring gap between the official language on ownership and actual practices in which, in the words of another participant 'international cooperating entities impose their priorities and models'. Participants acknowledged the decisive role played by international aid institutions in defining country strategies and cooperation programmes within the region, but stressed the importance of following up on how, in practice, aid programmes are actually designed and shaped by asymmetric power relationships.

What Kind of Financing for What Kind of Development?

The international trade system in its current form – especially Northern agricultural subsidies – is widely felt to represent an enormous obstacle to development in Latin America. In one-to-one discussions during the conference participants suggested that the North's current activities constitute 'a bipolar strategy': on the one hand, channelling resources to meet the MDGs, while on the other promoting an economic system for development that is anti-poor. They argued that discussion of how to finance development in Latin America cannot be separated from a deeper understanding of the current international context and the development paradigms it embraces.

CSOs and MDGs in Latin America

The literature indicates that Latin American CSOs generally view donor (and recipient government) commitments to the Millennium Development Goals (MDGs) as being of particular importance to their region because they offer an opportunity to fight poverty based on readily quantifiable and monitorable Indicators. However, conference participants voiced concerns over the fact that such targets may not adequately reflect the situation in the region – because MDGs fail to tackle the issue of inequality. A key reason for the region's disappointing performance to date, they argued, is that the main objective informing government policy has been excessively narrow. That is, policy has remained focused on accelerating growth, not on growth with equity. Relatively speaking, therefore, there has been minimal concern over income distribution or the social agenda, despite the fact that the region's income is more polarised than anywhere else in the world (with the exception of a few African countries). It may make sense, they pointed out, to focus policy overwhelmingly on growth in countries where income is less unequally distributed and the vast majority of the population is poor, like many countries in Africa. However, this is not the situation in Latin America where the elites are so rich relative to the masses that it is inconceivable that the living standards of the average person could ever be raised to acceptable levels through growth alone – i.e. without measures to narrow the gap between rich and poor. As one conference participant put it:

> 'A minor redistribution of income from the rich to the poor would have the same impact in reducing poverty as many years of growth with a constant income distribution, let alone of growth accompanied by further widening of the income gap.'

Other issues of growing concern to Latin American CSOs include government corruption and clientelism. CSO campaigns like the Latin American 'Global Campaign against Poverty' call for greater detail in donor commitments and greater coherence in their policies in order to address such issues. However, it is widely believed that donor policies and practices are not duly aligned either with the MDGs or with goals to promote social cohesion.

Bilateral assistance programmes were also considered unable to address the real needs of recipient countries in Latin America. Participants discussed how bilateral strategy papers were often produced with minimal input from Latin American actors, both governmental and non-governmental. Furthermore, despite the seemingly endless number of 'participatory workshops' convened, there was felt to be little transparency in the way that donor agencies function. Northern missions and experts play a decisive role in defining country strategy documents and cooperation programmes. Local participation and transparency is limited during consultations with domestic counterparts. The ownership-increasing effect of so-called 'participatory workshops or consultations' is widely discredited.

Latin American conference participants, like their counterparts in other regions, also complained of poor donor coordination and technical assistance despite the fact that this problem has gained increasing attention over the years. It was felt that donors needed to ensure that aid is untied and to develop better mechanisms for exchanging and sharing information. Technical assistance also inhibits attempts at strengthening country ownership of the development agenda. Despite progress in efforts to make aid more effective and flexible, bureaucratic requirements and transaction costs continue to be high. Donors need to continue to focus on channelling their assistance at the local level, where new and important political spaces have opened to empower citizens. The aid effectiveness agenda provides one opportunity for improving these matters, and platforms of Latin American NGOs (LANGOs) are joining the global CS effort for a more pro-poor Paris agenda.

Inefficiency remains a central issue in aid to the Latin American region. Despite all the debates and new policies on aid effectiveness, foreign aid remains very bureaucratic, procedures are too slow, and cooperation programmes take several years to be designed and executed. Subsequently, foreign aid programmes tend to have very high transaction costs. An army of foreign consultants, advisors and international officials consume much of the budget, displacing competent local professionals and using resources that should be allocated to development interventions. Even more disturbingly perhaps, the evaluation of aid programmes are frequently complex formal exercises.

In the last decade, relations between Northern and LANGOs have

Lower donor interest can be a blessing in disguise

undergone significant changes. It is not surprising that their common links and agendas have drifted further from each other. Traditional forms of association, i.e. partnerships have been severely strained and have been replaced by other, more pragmatic links. Radical changes have occurred in the world, which have provoked a crisis of the old paradigms of partnership and solidarity that previously inspired Northern and Southern NGOs. Both entities now face the challenge of defining a new common agenda and such new forms of intervention as development of global NGO platforms on issues of trade, human rights and the environment.

In short, Latin American civil society is strong, competent and vibrant – a fact which is also notable in its approach to M&E. The decline in donor interest in the region is, perhaps a blessing in disguise. The feeling among some workshop and conference participants was that the declining donor and INGO involvement in the region left more space for autonomy, self-determination and ownership.

INTRAC-Latin America Regional Workshop in Peru, 2005

In August 2005 an M&E workshop was held in Lima for CSOs active in the region. In the spirit of the open-ended conference methodology, the Peruvian workshop hosts were encouraged to choose their own issues of relevance. The event attracted considerable interest among local CSOs and sessions covered a wide range of topics including, amongst others, the evaluation of public policies in Bolivia, Peru and Costa Rica and the examination of the growth and emergence of networks in the Andean region and their future potential.

The seminar explored both the advances and challenges of M&E practice through contributions organised around the following topics: education; children and adolescents; public health; measurements of inequality in health; local and rural development; citizenship monitoring; M&E of research programmes about policy; institutional systems and organisational development and conceptual and methodological approaches. Conference participants exhibited a real interest in the introduction of new methodologies for enhancing the M&E capacity of staff.

The unexpectedly large attendance and enthusiastic participation of professionals in this conference is worth noting. Despite the absence of opportunities in terms of formal M&E education and training, the numbers of professionals in this field have increased significantly over the past five to ten years. The workshop was therefore perceived as an important means of bridging the gap between training and practice and was commended for promoting the exchange of experiences and availability of resources for M&E.

The Growth of M&E in Latin America

There appears to have been a growing concern and interest in M&E issues at all levels of civil society in Latin America. This is thought to originate in the basic desire for deeper analysis, good quality documentation of processes, results and impacts. However, a significant imbalance now exists between interest at the rhetorical level and the actual realisation of these goals.

LANGOs readily acknowledge that the effectiveness and impact of their interventions has not been what it should have been, and are now seeking more effective M&E measures as a means of ensuring more effective interventions. They have also made a point of requesting much more information and transparency about public policies. However, M&E at this level is still predominantly considered to be alien practice and LANGOs have engaged in it primarily as a reaction to such external demands. Although important progress was evidenced in M&E practices at the macro-level, institutional weakness and vulnerability were considered to be significant limiting factors. The desire of international agencies to have indicators and measurement systems (at a global level) contrasts with difficulties in the collation of national statistics and their aggregation.

At micro-levels, however, there is visible evidence of a gradual appropriation of M&E by local institutions. This interesting shift has been apparent since international NGOs have moved away from the region and that LANGOs are no longer under such intense external pressure. Participants were able to provide several examples where local organisations had developed their own M&E systems. This development was viewed as something that should be rooted internally and not arise from external pressure.

An important and very controversial debate at the sixth evaluation conference centred on the assessment of impact and effective indicators for this. This discussion had been preceded by a detailed discussion on the assessment of long-term, complex and participatory development processes within which power relationships were very evident and whose very characteristics would make long-term effects very difficult to predict. Participants reiterated that development is a complex process and that investment in capacity building in M&E tools and methodologies is needed for impact to be assessed effectively.

Linked to this discussion was also debate on the practice of participatory M&E, where the community take an active role and is at the centre of the evaluation. But the bureaucratisation of evaluation in Latin America hampers the implementation of participatory M&E. Indeed, M&E experiences presented during the seminar illustrated the diffusion and growth of M&E practices in both public and private organisations, with diverse uses of instruments and a myriad of lessons learnt.

Stumbling Blocks to Effective M&E Practice in Latin America

Characteristics of Latin American culture that were perceived as the greatest stumbling blocks to the effective design of M&E systems included unstable public service organisations (given discontinuity of staff); institutional weakness and the authoritarian attitudes that exist within many organisations. LANGOs, like agencies in other parts of the world, focus on activities but only minimally reflect on longer-term processes and strategic goals. Traits of organisational structure are difficult to modify and participants acknowledged the need for rapid cultural change within agencies.

Although there has been a gradual shift in emphasis from projects to programmes at the macro level there is as yet no clear process as to how to make this shift or indeed, how to link this shift with effective strategic planning. Moreover, a clear tension exists between the intense emphasis of many Latin American NGOs on human rights issues and that on service provision activities. Quantitative service provision type activities are always easier to measure. Related to this, participants highlighted the need for much more investment in capacity building around M&E tools and methodologies.

Conclusions

A detailed review of the Latin American literature on mechanisms for development delivery highlighted the following recommendations:

- Countries in the region should define a common agenda and collectively negotiate with donors.
- Projects should be substituted by programme aid and recipient-country priorities and needs should form the basis for informing such assistance.
- Latin American CSOs need to participate more actively in the process of defining development priorities, and local participation should be encouraged and strengthened more.
- The role of both Northern and LANGOs as watchdogs of official development assistance should not be neglected.
- It should be acknowledged and appreciated that NNGOs have played a key role in supporting and strengthening LANGOs, particularly in the fight against authoritarian regimes and support for human rights.
- As relations between Northern and Southern CSOs have severely declined, the key challenge for them is to attempt to establish a new agenda of renewed cooperation and find more equitable ways of relating to each another.

6

Europe: Between solidarity and fund management

Esther Mebrahtu and Linda Lönnqvist

Introduction

In recent decades the position of European NGOs has become painfully contradictory. European civic action for international development originated in idealism and solidarity but the current political climate and development policies places European-based NNGOs (Northern NGOs) on the same side as European bilateral donors. Direct budget support (DBS) and the aid effectiveness agenda[48] have channelled increasing amounts of bilateral aid straight to recipient governments, bypassing civil society actors. Moreover, across Europe, more conservative governments are being voted into office – many of which have lost patience with long-term, grassroots development programmes and are looking for what they believe to be more 'efficient' and 'quick fixes'. At home, donor governments are trying to

---

48. Direct budget support refers to the direct transfer of finance to the national or sectoral budgets of recipient countries. The aid effectiveness agenda refers to the process arising from a long campaign to streamline and harmonise aid, culminating in the Paris Declaration on Aid Harmonisation in 2005. Aid effectiveness deals with official development assistance (ODA) from bilateral and multilateral donors, tasking donors to harmonise their diverse practices and align aid with recipient country systems. It stresses managing for results, recipient country ownership of aid and mutual accountability between donors and recipients.

lower transaction costs by consolidating their funding for domestic civil society organisations (CSOs) in long-term funding agreements that favour the most prominent NGOs. The global counter-terrorism and security agendas are also seeping into development thinking, identifying NNGO offices based in developing countries more closely with the foreign policy of their home governments.

Meanwhile, the trend in recent years towards greater partnership and local ownership has compelled many NNGOs to stop delivering programmes themselves, relegating them to the position of donors whose principal aim is to channel funding to partner organisations. This has created a situation in which European NGOs are struggling to reconcile their ethos of solidarity and equal partnership with the increasingly urgent task of *cost-effectively* channelling funds to Southern organisations. This struggle is frequently reflected in general confusion over identity and consequently over adoption of M&E approaches which are able to effectively assess the quality of their programmes.

Setting the scene: The Wider Context Affecting M&E in Europe

The Mixed Blessing of 0.7%

Since the early 2000s, several European donor countries have made great strides towards increasing their level of overseas development aid (ODA). The official United Nations commitment for industrialised countries is that 0.7% of GDP should go to development aid. The '0.7%' and 'More and Better Aid' campaigns of recent years have had some success in persuading countries like Ireland to join the ranks of 0.7% donors such as the Netherlands, Norway and Sweden. Other EU countries have also increased their official aid budgets. Such increases, however, have not tended to include funding for more civil servants in development ministries. As a result, a shrinking number of donor ministry staff is now responsible for channelling the increased millions of ODA euros. The pressure for more cost-effective disbursement mechanisms is high. Indeed, DFID in the UK is currently investigating direct cash payments to poor people as a way of distributing aid funds. One can almost imagine politicians crying out in exasperation '... how can this be so complicated? Just GIVE them the money!'

This reality has made it necessary to focus on very large-scale programme funding such as DBS. Project-based, small-scale aid that can't demonstrate immediate and obvious impact is widely perceived as being too cumbersome for bilateral development agencies to administer. Many European countries have thus relegated funding for small-scale development activities to NGO umbrella organisations and large, well-established global NGOs. These same organisations then face the problem of how to undertake thorough and constructive M&E with increasing numbers of partners and projects. As this trend does not appear to be one that is likely to disappear in the near future, it really heralds the start of a strong demand for increased and more effective civil society (CS) activity in the South. The critical question that this poses is: where does this leave NNGOs? Or in other words: is there scope for more harmonised work with local CS actors?

From Food Security to National Security?

In the discourse of many European donors today, the terms 'poverty eradication', 'conflict' and 'peace' are increasingly intermingled with notions of 'terrorism' and 'security'. Research into the potential for aid to reduce the discontent of poor people and, hence, their likelihood to resort to violence has produced disappointing results. Indeed, one observation in the 'global terrorism' literature is that citizens are less interested in material welfare than in justice and autonomy. In short, even if aid managed to lift people out of poverty, some of them would still feel rightfully angry about global geopolitics.

Since it seems that more of the same aid won't be of much help in stifling violent tendencies worldwide, the aid discourse has started to change: now 'security' is beginning to be presented as a precondition for any material development. 'Security' is a longstanding development term, used to define stability and a dependable future in poor people's lives, e.g. food security. But the new use of security jargon is one that justifies the presence of soldiers and the military in development, i.e. national and internal security. The USA has reoriented its foreign policy to encompass 'the three Ds': diplomacy, defence and development, with increasing cooperation between the three. US NGOs are being approached by the armed forces with suggestions for collaboration, mostly in reconstruction and disaster management. Anecdotal evidence from Europe suggests that allies in the 'war on terror' are following suit.

As a result of this conflation of the development, Northern foreign policy, global security and anti-terrorism agendas, the integrity of development assistance for poverty eradication is at risk. The question appears to be: is development cooperation repeating its Cold War history of clientelism and once again becoming an extension of donor defence/foreign policies? The real impact of global geopolitics on aid allocations and the nature of donor cooperation with developing countries is only beginning to become apparent.

The Contested Ground of 'Ownership'

The 2005 Paris Declaration[49] established 'local ownership' as one of the central principles guiding the effective use of bilateral aid resources. Yet a closer examination of ODA belies this rhetoric. The Reality of Aid project[50] closely examines the nature of bilateral aid allocations in terms of its relevance to local ownership. It estimates that only 32% of total bilateral aid in 2004 was actually available to counterparts in developing countries as a resource they could allocate to implement their own development strategies. There was been a notable reduction from 39% in 2000, when donors pledged to spare no effort in a renewed partnership with developing countries. Developing country recipients therefore had a significantly smaller proportion of bilateral aid at their disposal in 2004, compared to a few years earlier, when they also had more control over the allocation of these funds.

Since 1992, Reality of Aid Reports have focused attention on the way in which aid has too often served donors' foreign policy and strategic interests, in turn ignoring and undermining the rights and needs of people living in poverty. They have also pointed to incremental progress in increasing the poverty focus of ODA since the late 1990s. But donors' self-interest and some recipient countries' misuse of aid have continued to undermine the potential for aid to contribute to poverty alleviation.

Thus, the wider European context includes shifts in aid priorities

---

49. www.oecd.org/document/18/0,2340,en_2649_3236398_35401554_1_1_1_1,00.html
50. www.realityofaid.org

towards efficient distribution, state-to-state aid and security, and away from activism, participation and poverty alleviation. This chapter attempts to understand how NGOs can get to grips with this changing aid architecture and resolve current obstacles so that it is possible to move towards a more productive use of M&E.

Themes Emerging from M&E Workshop in Härnösand, Sweden 2005

In the run-up to the sixth evaluation conference an M&E workshop was held in Härnösand, Sweden in March 2005. It was loosely aimed at exploring and identifying the emergent issues around M&E in European development agencies; the changing scope of M&E practice; the different types of approaches required to encompass such a change in shift and the key challenges that such a shift presents to current M&E practice.

Each day of the workshop was framed around a plenary session, followed by discussion groups which then reported back in plenary. The main topics were as follows:

- Day 1: Discussion groups were asked to report back on key challenges facing European development actors regarding the scope of M&E.
- Day 2: The focus shifted to challenges around the methods of M&E.
- Day 3: Participants were put in groups according to the type of actor (bilateral donors, NGO donor/partners etc.) and asked to put forward positive steps they could take to respond to some of the challenges.

The discussion groups were deliberately left open, in order to ensure that INTRAC staff did not steer the agenda, but rather enabled participants to bring forward the issues they faced within their work.[51]

Uncertainty over Role of European NGOs and Their Place in Aid Chain

The most immediately apparent emergent theme from this conference was the surprising level of ambiguity and even confusion expressed by Euro-

---

51. The feedback from participants suggested that this caused some frustration, as participants were keen to have more positive suggestions and details of new methods and approaches.

pean participants over the perceived role of their organisations within the new aid architecture. This confusion was initially observed when the following provocative question was posed by INTRAC: 'what is the added value of European NGOs?' In other words, why should donors continue to pass funds through these intermediaries rather than working directly with governments and NGOs in developing countries? Put in slightly harsher terms: would anyone other than INGOs notice if INGOs didn't exist? This was an extremely difficult question for many participants to answer with any level of certainty. However, as the aid architecture evolves the need to answer this question is likely to become increasingly pressing.

Interestingly, there was a slight geographic bias to the types of concerns registered by European participants. Western Europeans tended to be very critical of themselves and their ability to fulfil their mission statements. This group appeared to be struggling with their perceived dual roles as both civil society actors and as donors, and finding fault with their inability to employ M&E strategies that meet the needs of local partners. However, this duality of role was also perceived as 'strength' by other participants who viewed the role of NNGOs as that of a 'buffer' between large institutional donors and local NGOs and saw themselves as rights advocates.

Civil society actors from the former Soviet Bloc countries identified a completely different set of institutional concerns from their Western neighbours. Many of these had to do with recognition of the need to thoroughly break away from the historical centralist mindset. Dealing with the recent proliferation of donors in the region and their long list of administrative demands, and finding a unitary regional direction for their future programmes were also identified as primary concerns.[52]

Confusion was also expressed over how donor participants viewed their relationships with Southern NGOs. Indeed, there was an obvious reluctance to categorise their organisations' roles as being primarily that of donors – even though in many cases this would have been a more honest appraisal of the situation. Rather, the vast majority wished to view themselves as 'partners' or, more fashionably, as 'facilitators' in this relationship.

Implications of the Paris Agenda for the Role of Civil Society

Towards the latter part of the workshop, a presentation was made by a Sida official on the current progress of the Paris Declaration on the Aid Harmonisation agenda (discussed in chapter 2), to which many European governments had already subscribed. This provoked a highly controversial and lively debate. Many of the workshop participants, especially those from INGOs, realised that they had, up to this point, been almost entirely ignorant of the key premises on which this agenda was founded and its potentially far-reaching implications for their own organisations. One of the key revelations raised by the presentation was the extent to which the Declaration is premised on a narrow and highly restricted perception of CS within developing countries, which locates CS activities as conveniently fitting within the boundaries of national development plans. As such, the real significance of CSOs lies in their potential role as monitoring bodies for assessing how states implement PRSPs (poverty reduction strategy papers) and other formal processes.

This narrow interpretation of the role of CS was hotly disputed by conference participants primarily because it threatens to restrict the space for 'alternative' approaches to development that CSOs have worked so hard to get recognised. As Oliver Bakewell later pointed out in his summary of the

---

52. These and other such concerns are further discussed in chapter seven.

workshop:

> '... this puts European NGOs under even greater pressure to demonstrate their contribution if they are to successfully defend the space for creativity and diversity in approaches to development.'

Although nobody disputed the importance of even greater accountability on the part of CS, many felt it unfair that as a result of aid harmonisation the small space they had carved out for themselves over the years was yet again likely to be encroached upon by the state. One participant referred to this as 'a departure symbolic of going back to the 1980s'.

In addition, later discussions highlighted a myriad of other concerns held by CS participants. A few of these are presented below:

- Increased aid coherence through budget support implies greater 'ownership' over funds by Southern governments. Many Southern actors are frequently accused of corruption – a charge with potential to seriously undermine the credibility of the aid harmonisation agenda. How we mitigate this risk? What strategies have been put in place to minimise the likelihood? Bearing in mind that much CSO activity will have been subsumed under the umbrella of the state, how can such organisations continue to play an effective role as watch-dogs?

- Throughout the presentation of the Paris Declaration there was no mention of the link between this new agenda and the Millennium Development Goals (MDGs) towards the achievement of which so many development activities have been directed? Was the Paris agenda actually intended to support MDGs? If so, where are the indicators that can be used to assess this? Whose responsibility is it to ensure the two agendas and mutually reinforcing?

- Some participants complained about the highly mechanistic nature of the MDGs. They argued that the 'technical make-up' of the aid harmonisation agenda could lead future M&E programmes to be increasingly mechanistic in order to comply with the nature of the MDGs. If this happens, will there be space for the more in-depth client-based M&E approaches popularised in the 1990s and now widely accepted worldwide?

Although the majority of participants could be described as downcast, a few voices also highlighted the importance of recognising future potential opportunities that the Paris Agenda could offer. At the national level, the aid harmonisation agenda offers us an opportunity to strengthen local and central government through increased budget support. At the international level it provides an increased opportunity for INGOs to put pressure on their governments and more effectively hold them to account through less traditional channels, such as work with diaspora populations and work with the private sector. In other words, there is now pressure on both Northern and Southern CSOs to play a more vigilant and proactive role in order to ensure that:

- past lessons are not forgotten – such as the mistakes of the 1980s when the state was perceived to be the most dominant actor on the stage
- the public administration approach derived from this agenda does not further undermine downwards accountability on the part of key players
- we can prevent technocratic methods swamping client based participation
- we continue to learn from M&E activities (regardless of how quantitative/technical they may be in orientation).

All in all, the above discussion was instrumental in demonstrating that a great deal more debate/information exchange is required on the changing aid architecture and its potential impact on traditional CS roles.

As many participants were M&E practitioners by profession however, the key question they wanted answered is whether European NGOs still have a role in M&E in the new aid architecture. On first reflection, many participants felt their role would be greatly restricted as a result of such changes. However, as the debate developed it became increasingly apparent that European NGOs would have to reorient themselves in order to maintain their current relevance. As a starting step, participants felt they would have to become more 'comfortable in their skin as donors'. Only after reaffirming and clarifying their role as donors would they be able to effectively mobilise their Northern constituents (i.e. through planned advocacy campaigns and work with diaspora associations and the private sector) so as to help unite the North and South on critical issues. With the backing of the South, such NGOs could then legitimately play the role of intermediaries, as buffers, between large scale donors such as the EC and smaller organisations. Lastly, it was considered to be imperative that European NGOs remain sensitive to the wider global context, and that they budget appropriate time and money for actually learning from M&E initiatives.

Flexible Funding Stops with INGOs

Another highly controversial debate that took place among participants in both Sweden and the Netherlands was over institutional – or as we prefer to refer to it – 'flexible' funding.

Over the last decade European NGOs have been increasingly criticised for their failure to leave the micro-management of projects that they fund to the implementing (local) partners responsible for day-to-day operations. They have been accused of refusing to relinquish their complete control over such projects and of relegating local NGOs to the role of mere implementers. Participants queried why when such large scale official donors as the EC, DFID, Sida are gradually shifting the bulk of their funding towards large longer-term programmes, there are few signs to indicate that European NGOs are in turn passing on this type of flexible funding to their 'partners' in developing countries.

Participants pointed to a new and growing culture of contract-based relationships between donors and INGOs as a particularly extreme example of this countertrend. This point was well illustrated in day two of the conference when Tina Wallace presented a dramatic and disturbing case study of a popular UK-based NGO. It vividly demonstrated the potential difficulties of prioritising downwards accountability and learning (as good M&E practice dictates one should) when in a contract-based funding relationship with an official donor. Such experiences call into question the role of M&E in INGOs and why it is INGOs that undertake M&E? Are INGOs set to become become mere contractors to donor governments? If so, to what extent would this restrict the ëspaceí that currently exists for criticising donor activities and developing alternative and improved approaches?

When such concerns were raised, many participants denied that this scenario was a real and imminent danger for their particular INGOs. Others who saw their agencies had gone down this road warned, in the words of one participant, that:

'European NGOs are deceiving themselves if they think their organisations (and donors) are immune to the contract culture. This trend has only just began ...'

The failure to pass flexible funding on to partners appears to be symptomatic of current INGO-local NGO relations. The apparent reluctance of INGOs to free themselves and their partners of the highly criticised LFA (logical framework analysis) is just one case in point. Despite protestations from a number of official aid agencies who claim to have currently moved beyond requiring their recipients to use the LFA in their reports to donors, the principles of 'systematic LFA thinking' were something that many INGO representatives at the workshop felt they needed to maintain. Indeed, there was little evidence to support the claim that INGOs were finally moving away from the dominant types of M&E towards more client-based and context-specific approaches. The landscape of M&E, especially in the context of European NGOs, is still dominated by the LFA with few examples of SWOTs (i.e. 'strengths, weaknesses, opportunities and threats') analysis and participatory approaches. This undifferentiated use of tools, participants agreed, could not be good practice and lead many to question whether it is the LFA itself, or the 'method-thinking' it embodies, that has been the cause of so much of our current reservation.

So, why do so many European NGOs fail to pass on the advantages of more flexible (funding and reporting) mechanisms currently available to them? Examples, including Sida, no longer requiring LFAs, and several other European development ministries moving to long-term framework funding agreements with NGOs. Could it be that it is easier for INGOs to maintain the status quo, to continue to attribute the blame for difficult procedures onto donors rather than challenge their own funding and reporting mechanisms?

Accountability (or Accountancy) and Learning?

In the long-held tradition of all M&E conferences, there was a great deal of discussion over the tensions of attempting to address both accountability and learning within M&E practice. Participants agreed that, all too frequently, when accountability and learning are both identified as important criteria – for example, as part of the Terms of Reference for an evaluation –

learning is either completely neglected or poorly and ineffectively addressed. All too often, evaluations endeavour to address issues of accountability (e.g. for resources and activities) whilst setting aside any areas of learning as an 'assumed benefit' which users could decipher from the evaluation report at a later date. Unfortunately, this very rarely happens, especially with evaluations that do not explicitly address the need for learning.

Some participants debated the possibility of limiting their M&E efforts to monitoring only the use of resources i.e. basic financial accountability, so as to be able to invest more effort in evaluating levels of impact in a separate undertaking. As with much of the literature, many of these participants felt that there is currently too much emphasis on establishing elaborate, and often spurious, causal links between inputs and eventual impact. They wished to see these outputs disentangled from one another. Many felt the imperative to virtually force causal linkages had resulted from a historical over-reliance on the LFA as a starting point for many M&E initiatives. As Bakewell aptly put it (2006):

> 'a vicious cycle appears to have been established whereby INGOs feel they have to make exaggerated promises of what they can deliver, and the depth of impact this will have, in order to obtain higher levels of funding'.

When later requested to demonstrate that their programmes have achieved the desired effect, they tend to achieve this 'by claiming the credit for a significant number of the (positive) changes that have occurred within the life-cycle of the programme'. This then raises the frequently occurring problem of appropriate and accurate casual attribution. As participants acknowledged this recurrent dilemma, one suggested that future evaluations could perhaps focus on the 'plausible association' of contributions to impact, rather than on grand claims of proof that attributes impact to their work.

In an attempt to demonstrate how much effort had been expended within Sida on thinking through these very same issues of improved accountability attribution and learning, two Sida officials reported on current thinking within the agency. They explained how Sida was in the process of separating out their financial auditing systems (which focus on inputs and outputs – what the money has been spent on) from their more complex learning systems which tend to address questions of impact. This system, they explained, would enable Sida to separate monitoring for accountability at the lower levels of inputs and activities, from that undertaken (for the purposes of learning) at the higher levels of achievement of objectives and longer term impact.

While this idea seemed to resonate with a number of the participants at the workshop, there were a several key questions which they wished to address. For example, what new methods for M&E, if any, would this approach require? And could this be achieved through adapting current M&E methods which rely on the LFA? Although few would admit to being confident of the answers, there was a marked level of agreement with Bakewell's later statement that:

> 'there needs to be a radical pruning of the deadwood of existing M&E systems – especially the LFA – in order to enable new systems to be developed' (2006).

Something which became increasingly apparent from many participant discussions was that 'upwards' accountability is still the dominant paradigm within our organisations. The fashionable trend in favour of attaining 'downwards accountability' which we experienced in the 1990s appears to be once more on the wane. This is a challenge to us all. Although many donors don't appear to be interested in impact beyond the simplistic delivery of outcomes, it is important that we in the aid community continue to hold ourselves accountable to the clients on whose behalf we work.

Issues of how to manage the tensions between accountability and learning in M&E have been around for a long time. Yet the tension now seems to be at a level where we are beginning to question whether both accountability and learning can be addressed in any one M&E exercise, or whether they should be separated into two different exercises with clear criteria, methodologies and objectives.

The Importance of Learning in M&E

Despite the extensive literature declaring INGO aspirations to become 'learning organisations', there is little evidence to show this is happening. Once again, we note a gap between rhetoric and practice. As pointed out by Mebrahtu in her 2003 study of 10 UK-based INGOs working in Ethiopia (Mebrahtu, 2003), the commitment to learning at HQ, national and field levels seems to be frequently limited to that which does not throw up any real or 'embarrassing mistakes'. There is a desire for minimal change in the 'procedural status quo' so that managers may remain within their 'comfort zones'. Mebrahtu points out that it is the nature of learning that must ultimately lead to change. However, change is rarely, if ever, welcome. Indeed, for most people in their ordinary day-to-day lives, it is very unnerving to have to reflect deeply on their behaviours and activities! How much more threatening must learning seem amidst the complex political and developmental NGO agendas and ever-increasing demands on staff time?

Accepting human nature for what it is, it is easy to believe that, contrary to their rhetorical protestations, it may in fact not be in the interests of many agencies to *actually learn*. Invariably, competition for funding and enormous demands on staff time have significant impacts on potential for becoming learning organisations. We need to frankly acknowledge that learning is often sidelined because it is synonymous with change and human beings prefer to stick to familiar modes of practice.

Additionally, it is unfortunately often the case that learning from unsuccessful interventions far outweighs that which can be derived from those we consider 'successes'. Experience shows that 'learning from successes' often leads to the production of blue-prints. In an effort to recreate the success we invest heavily in the elusive search for that 'winning formula!' Consequently, even in an organisation which has minimal appreciation of upward accountability, learning from failure is only encouraged in 'safe spaces', away from prying ears. Nobody wants to admit to failure and nobody wants to admit that failure happens on their patch! Fortunately, there are some notable exceptions. ActionAid's attempt to undergo a major strategic transformation through its Accountability, Learning, Planning System (ALPS)[53] is one such example.

Legitimising Subjectivity

The current M&E systems in use by European NGOs tend to focus on pre-determined results which discourage social experimentation. As such, conference participants claimed, they are not appropriately designed to capture the complex change processes occurring in development interventions, many of which are characterised by the ambiguous, the intangi-

---

53. http://83.143.83.66/~actionaid/openinfo/pdf/revised.pdf

ble and the long-term. In attempting to monitor such changes therefore, participants emphasised the importance of *not* trying to capture the process in neat, predictable and logical boxes but rather, in describing them in qualitative terms. For this to be possible and for donors to consent to it, they claimed, both donors and INGOs would have to attach much greater significance to the 'informal, experimental and subjective'. As Mebrahtu has put it 'in a world where the often misguided notion of "objectivity" is king, we have to struggle to challenge orthodoxy and to legitimise "subjectivity"'[54]. There can be little doubt that this struggle is taking place in the dark recesses of many INGO offices today.[55] However, the pressures to act, achieve and count are likely to be overwhelming such efforts to understand analyse and learn (Wallace & Chapman 2005). Consequently, we have yet to find M&E systems that can capture the complexity and richness of the development experience. Until this occurs, perhaps the best we can do is to ensure that our current M&E systems do not reduce the bright colours of the development experience into a grey mush in an attempt to capture it in neat boxes.

Conclusion

At the start of this chapter, we described our aim as being to understand how INGOs as a sector can get to grips with the changing aid architecture and resolve current obstacles so that they can move towards a more productive use of M&E. At a global level we learned that significant levels of recent aid resources have been diverted for security purposes.

Recent aid pledges still fall far short of the urgently needed financing to meet even the minimal MDGS. Later this year, OECD-Development Assistance Committee (DAC) donors will be returning to a debate on expanding the criteria for ODA that could enable many to 'increase' their ODA

---

54. From a presentation by Esther Mebrahtu at the M&E workshop in Härnösand.
55. In the numerous debates on ways to capture the unintended consequences of development interventions there was a surprising level of interest around the 'Most Significant Change' (MSC) monitoring methodology. Developed by MS Denmark, MSC asks project participants what the most significant changes to their lives have been – positive or negative. At times, the most important changes related to a development intervention have nothing to do with the stated objectives. Peter Sigsgaard gives an example of an onion-growing project whose 'side effect' was to provide involved women with a voice and influence in their community.

through accounting adjustments. The European Community now has an opportunity to replace rhetoric and narrow self-interest with policies and resources that could truly make a difference and ensure that the next decade is devoted to ending global poverty and creating conditions for peace. As evocatively appealed in UNDP's 2005 Human Development Report: 'if ever there was a moment for decisive political leadership to advance the shared interests of humanity, that moment is now.'[56]

In spite of the major constraints imposed on INGOs by the new aid agenda – shifts in aid priorities towards efficient distribution, state-to-state aid and security and away from activism, participation and poverty allevi-ation – it is imperative that this sector continues to believe it has a critical and distinctive role to play. Now, more than ever, the CS community must hastily overcome issues of confused identity and role and determinedly act to change the rules of this new game. Drawing on the extensive lessons learnt from the past few decades, it has to be committed to highlighting (once again!) the importance of CS activism and participation in longñterm poverty alleviation interventions. Or failing this, perhaps accept its new role as a *shield* that local partners can employ to absorb the rigours of donor reporting requirements whilst they undertake the real business of bringing about change in the lives of the poor. If, in a more depressing scenario, it proves too difficult for INGOs to be sufficiently accountable and open to learning, the sector could agree to focus on fulfilling the minimum require-ments to maintain funding flows, but not expect M&E systems to provide useful learning. Whichever of the above paths is selected, one thing is cer-tain – European NGOs need to act rapidly in order to ensure their future role (in any capacity) on the development stage.

Areas for Improvement in M&E Practice

It has become glaringly apparent that current M&E systems in place within European NGOs are unable to cope with the numerous demands requested of them. In order to encourage ideas which could be used to redress this, one session within the European workshop was entitled 'How can we improve our current M&E systems?' The eight suggestions raised by

---

56. http://hdr.undp.org/reports/global/2005/

participants during this brief discussion provide a useful framework for improved M&E practice.

1. Rather than spending enormous amounts of time critiquing the work we do and the way we do it, perhaps we should try evaluating ourselves the way we do partners, placing greater emphasis on our organisational impact.

2. Oral evaluations can often work better for the purposes of internal assessments than written ones. This methodology should be further explored by donors.

3. 'Real time evaluation' is a new approach that deals with the problem that evaluations are only ever a snapshot in time. Real time evaluation is a longitudinal study often employed within disaster management by organisations such as the World Food Programme. It enables evaluators to build up trust and relationships with local people over a longer period of time and is far less formal.

4. European NGOs need to be allowed by donors to change strategies and, for example, to move away from the current over-emphasis on the use of MDG indicators. The way these indicators are used is also too mechanical and must be better interpreted.

5. There is a clear need for more comparative work across agencies to avoid duplication of effort and waste of resources. Agencies could share the cost of baseline data and share secondary data from different contexts. Better co-ordination is needed for data sharing between agencies.

6. Tools such as the LFA have become easy scapegoats for some bad M&E practice. This tool does work as long as it is used flexibly. We need to use it with more innovation and recognise its shortcomings (e.g. assumption/risk elements are often ignored and there is little room for in-depth analysis).

7. Gaining the commitment of frontline staff is a key issue in improving M&E practice. If staff are interested, and feel a sense of ownership of data they are collecting, they are likely to do a better job.

8. If united, agencies need not be afraid to challenge orthodoxy with regards to M&E practice. Combining and reconfiguring a range of existing qualitative methods was suggested as one way of helping to legitimise more subjective methodologies.

7

M&E Tensions, Challenges and Future Opportunities

Esther Mebrahtu

This chapter brings together similarities and differences between the five regions included in the sixth evaluation conference. In an attempt to draw lessons from these comparisons and highlight future opportunities the chapter analyses the major tensions and challenges to M&E practice – a key constraint being the way aid is increasingly directed towards central governments.

Common Wider Thematic Issues Emerging

Over the years we have observed that evaluation conferences tend to reflect wider topical debates, thus illustrating how M&E issues mirror the development discourse in which they are situated. A number of wider thematic issues emerged from this regional survey of M&E questions. We were interested to note that although there were significant differences between (and within) the various regions, there was an undeniable confluence of opinions on a number of broad issues which shall be discussed in turn below.

Rediscovering the State: Back to the 1980s?

The new aid harmonisation agenda signals a global trend towards a more technocratic, bureaucratic and state-centred view of bilateral development aid. It appears that the state, after having been discredited as a worthwhile development institution throughout the 1980s, has been rediscovered. 'Good governance' is once again the name of the game and is being rewarded with higher levels of bilateral aid on an increasingly unconditional basis – such as direct budget support, sector wide approaches, the Millennium Development Goals (MDGs), design of Poverty Reduction Strategy Papers (PRSPs) and aid alignment. In these debates, scepticism about states and concerns about corruption are counterposed to capacitation and absorptive capacity thinking. Meanwhile the role of civil society (both in the North and South) appears to have been relegated to that of ensuring that the state remains accountable through democratic processes, (including popular M&E) and continues to fill gaps left by the state and market. Hence civil society organisations (CSOs) have once again been assigned the shallow and undesirable task of providing welfare and/or more recently been consigned to the role of sub-contractors complementing existing state-provided social services.

The 'Boiling Frog' Danger

While the aid harmonisation agenda gains momentum, both Northern and Southern civil society has largely remained on the margins of serious policy discussions about it. Donor coordination platforms have not sought active CSO participation nor viewed civil society as critical to this agenda. Neither does it feature in any significant way in the Paris Declaration.[57] A brief review of the literature reveals that recent aid architecture debates have not featured prominently in the agenda of Northern and Southern CSOs during the first 18 months following the Paris Declaration, although CS engagement has gathered momentum since then.

Questions as to why this should be the case and identification of the reasons why CS appears to be on the fringes of significant aid policy discussions, were posed intermittently throughout the sixth evaluation conference but without much success.[58] However, one participant's explanation seemed to hit home and evoked a great deal of spontaneous agreement. He suggested

---

57. www.oecd.org/document/18/0,2340,en_2649_3236398_35401554_1_1_1_1,00.html
58. The legitimacy of non-government actors in policy formulation is a longstanding debate in political science. Civil society does make valuable policy contributions, and although CS lobbying strength varies considerably, there is no reason not to maximise advocacy opportunities.

that marginalisation of civil society actors as a whole was in fact typical of a strategy more popularly known as the 'boiling frog syndrome'. Pressed to explain his point, he pointed out that if one wishes to boil a frog, the worst strategy is to simply throw the frog into boiling hot water, since it would only jump straight out of the pan. Instead, the frog should be placed in warm water and the heat steadily increased, thus boiling the frog without the animal realising the danger it is in – until it is too late.

Within the context of the changing aid climate, the participant suggested that critical Paris Declaration policy decisions had been agreed without active CS participation as part of a deliberate strategy to exclude CSOs from decision-making fora.[59] This belief was substantiated by our finding that few (if any) of the European participants at the Härnösand workshop were even aware of the Paris Declaration and other critical changes to the global aid environment being negotiated at the time. The boiling frog metaphor therefore effectively alerted CSOs to the need to learn about and engage with high-level policy debates while there is still a possibility of exerting influence – before the water in the pot becomes uncomfortably hot!

NGOs must stay alert to gradual changes in the global aid climate – or be caught unawares.

59. As noted earlier, the Paris Agenda – a code of conduct for aid donor and recipient countries – excludes CS participation and has serious implications for CS.

Is the Security Agenda Swamping Development Concerns?

With the escalating post 9/11 prioritisation of the security agenda questions are being asked of the international community's commitment to poverty reduction and the quality of future aid.

As donors have become increasingly preoccupied by perceived security threats, focused ever more on security sector reform, fragile states and post-conflict reconstruction and allocated ever greater resources to the 'war on terror', the gap in funding required to realise commitments to achieving the MDGs has become ever starker. Donor policies and aid allocations have started to focus on an expanding security agenda in the South, accompanied by overt diversions of aid resources to regions of the world that are seen to threaten security in the North or to counter-insurgency activities in zones of conflict. Furthermore, humanitarian assistance and reconstruction efforts following the wars in Afghanistan and Iraq have captured more than a third of aid resources allocated by donors since 2001.[60]

Participants at the Netherlands conference voiced major misgivings about this state of affairs and unanimously agreed with the statement of a European donor official that 'we run the risk of obliterating all that we've achieved [as regards poverty alleviation programmes] if this trend continues'. What was perhaps more disappointing was the general feeling of powerlessness exhibited by many participants during such discussions. Despite the disheartening reversal of aid trends described above, participants appeared listless – it was almost as if the issue of 'security' was 'too hot a potato' to really explore.

Wider Issues Emerging around M&E Practice

A key observation made by previous conference organisers during this sixth series conference was that the general discourse on M&E seems to have fragmented into two camps. In the 1990s both donors and implementers appeared to have reached an unspoken consensus on the desirability of using people-centred, rather than technocratic, M&E approaches. The client-focused school of thought had finally won! However, recent trends

---

60. Reality of Aid 2006 report:
http://www.realityofaid.org/roareport.php?table=roa2006&id=1

in global aid policies appear to have been reversed. New thinking among key decision-makers de-emphasises participatory principles and methodologies, focussing instead on a more minimalist view of development that tends to dismiss the significance of impact.

As long-time devotees of the participation ethos espoused by Robert Chambers from as far back as the 1980s, conference organisers consider it a great pity that the struggles waged back then by NGOs in favour of a more populist view of development may have to be re-fought in the face of more technocratic trends. That this is necessary is doubly unfortunate considering that virtually all development practitioners now believe in the effectiveness of a more participatory view.

In attempting to explore some of the reasons for this fragmentation, we were able to identify three contributing factors.

The first relates to the *confusion about identity* uncertainty whether their primary role is that of development worker, activist or donor – shown by European donors in the Sweden workshop. This muddling of roles has, unsurprisingly, also coloured perceptions over M&E function, for the role of an agency in M&E will vary depending on its role in the overall development process. This connection may seem commonsensical but is not readily made by everyone. In part this is because of a genuine confusion, but it also emanates from a tension between the roles people want to play (facilitator, partner, co-worker) as opposed to those they are institutionally obliged to play (donor, accountant, middle-man etc).

A second contributory factor relates to the current fixation with 'greater efficiency' in disbursement and operationalisation of aid funds. This drive has been coupled with an attempt to down-grade monitoring to a low priority activity, and reduce evaluation to a 'bag counting' form of minimal accountability. This de-prioritisation of M&E is also symbolised by the physical marginalisation of evaluation departments within many donor organisations – DFID's evaluation department situated in Kilbride, Scotland being a case in point!

Thirdly, fragmentation of the M&E discourse can be attributed to significantly *changed relations between Northern and Southern NGOs* which has resulted in fewer common points of interest. Traditional forms of association and partnership have been severely challenged by current realities and have been replaced by other, more pragmatic links. Radical changes in the world have provoked a crisis of the old paradigms of partnership and solidarity that previously inspired Northern and Southern NGOs. Both sets of institutions now face the challenge of defining a new common agenda and new lines of intervention. An example is developing global NGO plat-forms/networks on issues of trade, human rights and the environment.

Three other less controversial changes observed in M&E discourse and practices at a wider contextual level are listed below:

Does the Current Aid Agenda Herald the Death of Impact?

One very notable change within M&E discussions and literature at an international level in the past five years has been reduced attention to issues of impact and impact assessment methodologies. We have observed a reversion to strict, mostly quantitative M&E systems, often limited in scope to measuring what activities have been delivered against plans. As mentioned above, the 'greater efficiency' debate has been used to justify this trend. However, this focus on efficiency has ended up blurring the line between 'efficiency' and 'effectiveness' – so much so that at times the two terms are now used synonymously. This neglect of impact and effectiveness is of particular concern when viewed within the context of budgetary sup-port and sector-wide approaches that have been introduced with techno-cratic forms of M&E – the key role of which should be to confirm that such measures are actually beneficial to poor people.

Such approaches are requirements of the growing sub-contract culture between donors and implementers, but can often lead to extensive atten-tion being focused on the demonstration of compliance with deliverables, and very little effort expended on the review of outcomes and/or impact. Answering the 'so what' questions related to impact, requires the use of a range of client-focussed M&E approaches that go well beyond assessing the attainment of delivery targets. However, because of the time and resource-intensive nature of such approaches there must be strong incentives to encourage meeting longer-term targets before such methods would be read-ily employed. Without such structures, it will be all too easy for us to focus on short-term targets and ignore the critical question of impact.

Downward Accountability

The steady decline of *projects* with defined boundaries and timelines in favour of longer term *programmes* has meant that M&E methods have had to struggle to be appropriate to the more ill-defined, or at least very broadly-defined, outcomes of recent poverty alleviation programmes (such as 'strengthening civil society' and 'the empowerment of women'). It has been difficult to engage with PRSPs and other such intangible processes. In the midst of their struggle against increasing marginalisation by a development model which assumes state leadership, CSOs have been increasingly frustrated by the co-option of critical concepts which form the foundations of their roles and activities. Over the last decade for example, the principle of participation has been presented with an instrumentalist focus (rather than as part and parcel of the empowerment principle) so as to ensure that people buy into programmes externally designed by the World Bank, bilateral agencies and some larger NGOs. Thus, although there are now more opportunities for M&E to be used by citizens to monitor government performance (budget monitoring, local democracy etc), for the most part the emphasis on M&E as a means of strengthening accountability (especially downwards accountability) has seen a gradual decline. In an increasingly competitive funding environment, if donors do not make this an *explicit* requirement for further funding the important principle of downwards accountability is likely to fall by the wayside and slide into oblivion.

Poor Donor Coordination and Technical Assistance

Poor donor coordination, low-quality technical assistance and general inefficiency remain key impediments of aid to developing countries. Despite recent talk of aid harmonisation and new policies on aid effectiveness, foreign aid remains very bureaucratic, procedures are too slow and cooperation programmes take several years to be designed and executed. Foreign aid programmes have thus tended to have very high transaction costs. As one means of redressing this issue, donors need to continue to focus on channelling their assistance at the local level, where new and potentially important political spaces may exist to empower citizens.

Regional M&E Issues Emerging

Bearing in mind that so many changes are afoot at the global level of aid and M&E debates, it was interesting, albeit slightly disheartening to note during the sixth conference the major disconnect between these issues and those pinpointed by development staff working on the ground. For many development workers, the aid harmonisation agenda seems to bear little relevance to their own efforts at assessing their own work. The fact that we are being slowly driven into M&E at the level of activities and outputs rather than outcomes and impact, (i.e. caught in the trap of not thinking about and addressing the bigger picture) was as yet not evident from the conference discussions of those working at field level.

Questions remain as to why development workers do not relate their struggles with M&E practice to changes occurring in the global aid system. Why do many appear to view the international aid architecture as an exogenous variable over which they have little control? This oversight often reflects the low interest of many CSOs in engaging with high-level policy issues in the face of the pressures to 'get the job done'. Lack of exposure, accentuated by their marginal participation in global platforms, has obviously limited the capacity of many CSOs to make this link. Thus, there is an ever-widening gap between those directly engaged in development, and those responsible for accountability to resource providers. This is a serious issue that should have been considered during the regional workshops and conference.

The types of M&E issues that were more prevalent during regional discussions included those most frequently quoted at almost every international M&E forum. A selection of these is listed below:

The Search for the 'Holy M&E Grail'

Perhaps the most frequent observation to emerge from the regional workshops was what we jokingly coined 'the desperate search for the holy M&E grail'.[61] The term is apt, for there appears to be an ever-present oft-recurring belief among participants in the existence of a 'new' M&E approach that

---

61. According to Christian mythology, the Holy Grail is the dish supposedly used by Christ at the Last Supper. The quest for the elusive Holy Grail is central to legends associated with King Arthur. The phrase is used to denote any aspiration for an ultimate or perfect solution to a problem.

can be deployed in any emergency, advocacy campaign or service delivery programme. Belief in the existence of this tool 'somewhere out there' was particularly evident at the Netherlands conference where participants never ceased to ask for new M&E publications with new and effective tools. Although the sixth conference was a 'master-class' M&E event discussing the wider issues around M&E, the methodology toolkit used for that conference can be found in Appendix 1 for readers of this volume.

It is easier to search for newer and more exciting tools than to apply ourselves to the nitty-gritty of M&E.

Requests were frequently made for INTRAC professionals to recommend one methodology over another within a particular context, e.g. for assessing advocacy campaigns. The introduction of 'citizen monitoring' as a methodology was greeted with the same buzz as 'the most significant change' methodology had commanded in the fifth evaluation conference. It was disappointing to note that this extensive interest in the next 'wonder tool' masked a continuing belief in the 'it's the tool you use and not the way you use it' philosophy which many of us had hoped to have left behind in the 1990s. The idea of a 'new tool' can often become a mental crutch that people lean on, wrongly assuming that they need it. And this can frequently lead to impeding the progress of further reflection and learning.

Is it a Case of 'Old Wine in New Bottles'?

During the regional workshops many new and interesting ideas were identified and explored. However, one set of questions were repeatedly posed by a disturbing number of participants: 'Are we grappling with the same M&E problems as previously identified in previous M&E conferences?'; 'are we moving beyond the log frame?' and 'are we moving beyond accountability to learning?' The evidence would appear to suggest not. This issue is more closely examined in the concluding chapter.

Beyond 'us and them' – NGOs and donors

The perceived institutional barriers to innovative practice in M&E led to much debate during regional workshops around the 'us' versus 'them' dichotomy. Those higher up the aid chain were seen as responsible for the problems lower down the chain. We were surprised to learn, when all participants were later gathered in the Netherlands, that many of the constraints perceived by those lower down the chain were actually self-imposed – and nothing at all to do with 'donor tyranny'! For example, the widespread use of the much maligned Logical Framework Analysis (LFA) had frequently been attributed to the requirements of donors. Yet several donor representatives at the conference fervently denied this, insisting that they had given their partners a selection of report formats from which the partner had themselves selected the LFA. When later questioned about this, many of the partner organisations explained that they had selected to use the log-frame as they had believed this to be the 'weapon of choice' for most donors.

This discussion inevitably brought about a much more in-depth debate on the issue of trust. Indeed, institutionalising trust into M&E practices was the subject of numerous discussions both during workshops and the conference. The vicious cycle of over-inflated expectations and incentives to report only successes has made trust between such actors extremely difficult. This is a problem which must be resolved if we are to ever move forward with M&E practice.

Future Regional Opportunities for M&E Practice

While much of the preceding discussion has focussed on the common tensions and challenges faced by M&E practitioners, the following section seeks to highlight some potential opportunities that exist for increasing the effectiveness of M&E practice. As each region has its own very unique context these opportunities are discussed within each specific geographical boundary.

Latin America

Latin American participants affirmed the rising interest in M&E in the continent. This is evidenced, they claim, by the gradual appropriation of M&E principles and practices by local institutions – an event that has curiously coincided with the departure of many INGOs from the region. Freed from the rigorous and draining reporting often imposed by donors, participants highlighted several examples where local organisations had taken the momentous decision to develop their own context-specific M&E systems to service their own requirements. This advance provides a great opportunity for the principles and methods of M&E to be internalised, strengthened and developed within a locally appropriate context.

Asia

The widespread rise in the popularity of the citizen monitoring methodology[62] provides a key opportunity that could be exploited for the purposes of strengthening citizen-led advocacy campaigns. Furthermore, the use of this methodology has increased interest in more in-depth analytical processes and greatly heightened the focus on impacts. As such, citizen monitoring provides the perfect platform for putting M&E-related issues

---

62. A methodology widely perceived to be an empowering tool for strengthening citizen participation, accountability and promoting transparency within governance institutions.

back on the Asian map. What is still missing however is the capacity to systematically compile, document, analyse and put into practice the substantial learning that frequently results from using citizen monitoring.

In latter discussions of appropriate M&E methods for use within humanitarian emergencies, the role of the media (and digital media in particular) was flagged as being of great potential significance if used to supplement and assist local CSO assessments of such crises. The media is, undoubtedly, the greatest source of information at many levels: it can highlight the level of destruction, indicate the needs of the disaster region and its people, show how they are being met (or not met) and maintain pressure on governments and the humanitarian community by keeping the story of the emergency alive. The media thus constitutes a potentially untapped resource for use within the assessment of humanitarian disasters.

Europe

The apparent lack of a clear consensus on the identity, roles and responsibilities of European NGOs is a challenge to all of us working in development, especially M&E practitioners. However, this situation does also afford such organisations the opportunity to stop, re-trace their steps and seek to clarify and comprehend their own roles and that of M&E within their own organisations. The very fact that some European INGOs are now beginning to question the added value of their existence also means that such donor organisations are becoming more flexible to the idea of 'loosening up' on their reporting requirements. Southern CSOs should now seek to exploit the space this may have created to negotiate with donors on the use of such tools as the LFA. They may even have the opportunity to select and introduce donors to formats they feel to be most effective in their own contexts.

Central Asia

Central Asian and other nations which emerged from the former Soviet Union add a valuable and fresh dimension to the traditional concept of 'development'. Central Asian participants insist that the term should either be enriched or expanded, to better encompass the different realities of their region, or dropped altogether. This has afforded some regional CSOs the opportunity to attempt to re-configure 'development' to better reflect their own reality. In so doing, they have also been able to innovate and develop more locally appropriate methods for undertaking M&E.

While the participatory ethos is weak, and analytical (including M&E) capacity is still in its relative infancy, this region could still surprise itself and the rest of the world. A complex history may have made it difficult for Central Asia CSOs to immediately find their place in either mainstream or alternative civil society forums globally. However, the fact that the geopolitical interests of leading centres of global development – the USA, Russia, China and the Islamic world – intersect in Central Asia means that the region now has a '... chance to mediate on the crossroads between the largest mega-regions' (Moldesheva & Buxton, 2006:2).

Africa

In the world of M&E, tensions continue to exist between formal and informal methods, between scientific and anecdotal evidence and between subjective and objective findings. The workshop in Ghana demonstrated that Africa is a continent which, more than any other, is torn between different approaches. With Africa's great history of oral traditions the continent's NGOs struggle to legitimise, and to obtain official recognition, of long-established cultural practices. Although traditional oral techniques such as 'story telling' can (and frequently do!) capture the complexity and richness of development experiences without reducing the experience into the 'grey mush' often resulting from conventional methods, Africans struggle to persuade donors of the legitimacy of the 'subjective' evidence they produce.

However, there is a ray of hope. Across the globe donors are increasingly accepting less formal M&E approaches. Few could argue that they are unaware of the increasing popularity and utilisation of approaches such as 'Most Significant Change', 'Appreciative Enquiry' and 'Outcome Mapping' in modern day programmes. This broadening of opinions provides an excellent backdrop and opportunity for African NGOs to resume their fight to legitimise established cultural practices.

Conclusion

The aid effectiveness agenda in its currently form threatens to marginalise the role of CSOs and may ultimately result in eroding the democratic space for voicing dissent that such organisations have carved out for themselves over the last three decades. It is thus imperative that civil society groups themselves take on the responsibility of protecting and defending their value base and independence.

As Brian Pratt pointed out in his closing remarks at the sixth evaluation conference, however, this move requires more courage and commitment to their own ideas than many organisations currently display. Those who have stood up for what they believe in, and experimented with different approaches, are still with us. However, we need to ensure that space is protected to allow flexibility. We must not let innovation be swamped by a deafening uniformity which satisfies neither clients nor the donor agency staff whose work is constrained by it.

8

Towards a Conclusion or a New Start?

Brian Pratt

Introduction

In preparing for the *Sixth International Conference on Monitoring and Evalua tion* we wanted to raise the big questions that practitioners were facing but we did not want to be directive by setting the key issues in advance. Thus we decided to take a more open approach to the workshop and conference methodology. Rather than dictate what we saw to be the priorities and issues, we agreed to find the resources to provide space for open discussions and for issues to emerge.

After the conference, the steering committee responsible for the sixth conference met to review: whether we had succeeded, the issues raised, the questions asked and what subjects and suggestions had been well-received and which had not.

The regional workshops raised a number of questions which were then taken to the international conference. Here the open methodology allowed tensions to emerge between the concerns and preoccupations of the different international stakeholders. As we analysed these issues we began to see that there were actually a number of bigger and more fundamental questions emerging from behind a smoke screen of rhetoric and discussion over what, at the end of the day, are often rather less important but more overtly apparent tensions.

Why is it that a number of issues seem to keep haunting the debate?

'Over nearly two decades the *same old questions* keep recurring'. This comment keeps being heard at conferences and meetings on M&E. If this is the case, what is holding us back from improving the situation and learning from the accumulated wisdom or lack of it?

We have witnessed endless repetition of questions about logical frameworks, management systems, participation, accountability and learning, and rather fruitless debates on whether one is superior to another or whether qualitative or quantitative methods are best. Are we going around in circles because we do not want to challenge our way of doing things? Is it easier to stay in the 'comfort zone' with ideas and practices with which we are unhappy, but familiar? Are development institutions frightened of more open debate on what worked and what did not? Is evaluation only popular when we need some evidence to show that a previous ideologically-based development theory or paradigm can now be discredited? Are we loath to ask too many difficult questions about the latest fashionable theory or approach? Are the institutional imperatives for good or bad news according to prevailing prejudices driving the M&E profession (if we can call it that)? If so, this would not be very flattering about many of us in this field! We would, no doubt, be able to pass the blame to our managers and those who commission us to do evaluations and who set the parameters for our work. If this is the cause of our dilemma, this probably shows that we need to understand how M&E fits within the development of both organisations, and the agreed consensus of the different sectors and communities within the aid business.

Although many would like to see M&E as a set of approaches and processes which stand alone and can be adapted for a multitude of needs – from the smallest community group to the largest trans-national organisation – the reality we are facing is that most M&E has become dominated by the needs of the aid industry and its range of key stakeholders. Even where we argue for client-based M&E this is, unfortunately, often picked up and endorsed by major stakeholders more out of a desire to influence other agencies than from a genuine desire to listen to and act on the opinions and feelings of clients.

In debates at the fifth conference on the tensions between participatory techniques and organisational based management M&E systems we saw how there is a confusing divide – even within individual organisations – between these different and competing demands. The mythology that M&E is somehow neutral and immune to these demands hinders ability to design and implement M&E systems and to analyse their products. In other words, far too much M&E work is dominated by short-term organisational imperatives, rather than a genuine interest in either accountability or learning or a real commitment to ensuring that development interventions actually lead to socio-economic change.

Differing perspectives

In the processes of discovery, analysis and discussion represented by the workshops and conference it became increasingly obvious that there were some very different perspectives between the donor communities (NGO and official agencies) and the recipient countries and institutions. It would be tempting to call this a North-South divide, but that would be too simplistic. For it also became clear that there are some very different perspectives within each of these rather ill-defined geographic categories.

Were these differences significant or not? In trying to separate out what seems to be creating the divide we can identify several key elements. Two of the most pertinent are:

- a new move on the part of NGOs to being more operational: this often, but not invariably, entails the delivery of contracted services for either donors or sometimes governments.
- a tendency to embrace a short-term view of results-based management instead of a commitment to longer-term social change.

Those agencies who have moved into operational work (many Northern or INGOs have changed their way of working recently) and subcontracting (which applies to both Northern and Southern organisations) find themselves increasingly driven by the need to show that they have met obligations around pre-set deliverables. The common management response to the 'tyranny' of deliverables is to adopt tighter results-based systems. In themselves these might not be a problem, but as those who deliver these services distance themselves from longer-term responsibilities they choose to translate the deliverables into short-term compliances with specific inputs and activities. Thus they abnegate responsibility for the eventual outcomes and impacts of their work, assuming these to be the responsibility of the contracting agent, not themselves.

The consequence for M&E is a focus on the short-term and on the 'tools' which will enable the assessment of compliance against agreed deliverables. There is a resurgence of interest in the 'tools' and methodologies to monitor and report on the activities achieved as defined by signed agreements. The key terms are 'measurement', 'management' and 'control'. Even where an agency has its own funds (not contracted) they also then adopt these techniques although there is no need to do so. This avoids a situation whereby the organisation is trying to run simultaneously with two or more systems and approaches.

The end result is a culture where the achievement of short-term objectives in terms of activities becomes the norm and where an increasing number of development agencies are moving away from an interest in the impact of their work and thereby the desire to assess whether they have been successful in achieving their overall goals/objectives. Where the interest in longer-term impacts or social change are in decline we should not be surprised that it becomes more difficult to then rate the value of an agency except in terms of the efficiency of their management system, rather than whether their interventions and actions are effective. We have seen in our discussions of official agencies that they are also stuck in the trap of confusing efficiency – including improved public administration and reduced corruption – with effectiveness in terms of actually improving services or reducing poverty.[63] As development agencies become aware that the greatest criteria to judge their performance is efficiency, not effectiveness, they will understandably focus on improvement in the former. And the evidence is that many of the agencies which are growing are those which project and sell an image of efficiency as contractors. Thus contracts are awarded to those who apparently deliver and on time regardless of whether

---

63. ONTRAC 33, (May 2006), 'Aid Harmonisation: Challenges for Civil society' www.intrac.org/docs.php/69/Ontrac_33.pdf

what is delivered has actually had any impact on the client/recipient population.[64]

At the same time many agencies are still struggling to understand how best to achieve their goals. At regional workshops concerns were expressed about how to:

- further address the challenges of assessment of advocacy initiatives especially in Africa and South Asia
- address the issue of 'citizen monitoring' (Latin America and South Asia)
- measure whether a community has been empowered
- assess whether humanitarian responses have built or destroyed local capacity (South Asia)
- determine whether more women have become engaged with local community-based organisations.

The list is endless and further examples can be found in the previous chapters. Perhaps we should not be surprised that those grappling with difficult questions such as these are more concerned to have M&E systems which delve beyond the short-term 'efficiency' of their delivery to the longer-term impact of their work. There is a recognition that many of these questions cannot be answered in the short-term until the processes have been completed which is often long after the end of the specific externally-funded intervention.

For a number of Southern partners in particular there is a feeling that a preoccupation with tools and methodologies is acting as a straitjacket to innovative thinking. Some argue that these constraints are a result of an increasing move towards micro-management by Northern NGOs of their Southern partners, whilst others see that a move towards accepting contracts from local government reduces space for innovation.[65]

Monitoring and evaluation in many NGOs continues to focus on the *micro-management* of projects rather than leaving this to the partners who

---

64. The current weakness of evaluation departments in both multi and bilateral agencies removes the ability to carry out impact evaluations.

65. Alikan F, Kyei P, Mawdsley E, Porter G, Raju S, Townsend J., Varma R. (2007) shows how very many developing country NGOs are also becoming dominated by the contract-for-services culture.

are responsible for implementation and day-to-day operations. As some government donors are however, moving towards more programme funding and stepping back from the details of individual projects, there are still few signs that European NGOs are passing on this flexibility to their 'partners' in developing countries.[66]

This comment reflects the unfortunate tendency to adopt restrictive approaches to funding even where this is not necessary due to more flexible funding on the part of some donors in Europe. It suggests that the new industry standard is better suited to contracting rather than more reflexive forms of social development. One clear step towards regaining our ability to improve our understanding of the real impact of our work should be to at least loosen the hold of short-term management models where these are not considered a necessary requirement by donors, and where in reality they are contributing very little to the ability of the organisation in question to manage their own work.

What is the link between learning and accountability?

The second major issue which continues to divide and obstruct our attempts to improve M&E practice are questions to do to with the old *debate about learning and accountability:*

- Are they separate?
- Is it time for a divorce (or at least an amicable separation)?
- Can some evaluations only deal with one or the other?
- What are the implications for M&E of such a separation?

These issues were raised in the European workshop and produced several suggestions of how to answer them. There is a general understanding from those involved in M&E that when accountability and learning are put together – for example as part of the Terms of Reference for an evaluation – learning is often left out or not addressed clearly/effectively. Too often an evaluation will address the issues of accountability for resources or activities and leave learning as an 'assumed benefit' which users of the evaluation will be able to make at a later date. The reality is that all too often this

---

66. Excerpt from the European Workshop Report

does not happen with the majority of evaluations, which do not explicitly addressing learning. This is made even worse when external consultants are used. They have the most potential to learn from such an event and are actually paid to walk out of an organisation with this potential knowledge!

A few agencies are exploring the possibility of limiting monitoring to the use of resources at the level of basic financial accountability and investing more effort in M&E at the level of impact. This idea looks at the different levels of M&E and focuses monitoring for accountability at the lower levels of inputs and activities and learning at the higher levels of achievement of objectives and longer-term impact.

The issue of how to manage the tensions between accountability and learning in M&E has been around for a long time. Yet it now seems to be at a level at which we have to ask the question 'Can learning and accountability be addressed in one evaluation or should they be separated into two different exercises with clear criteria, methodologies and objectives?' Has our problem been that we have been trying to reconcile two very different perspectives and ending up not satisfying either? Lessons from practice would often appear to conclude that is the case. And yet what would happen if we de-linked the two? Would we be better off or would the gains and clarity be short-lived? Is the difference between learning and accountability as clear as we are making out?

In the aid industry we often have very long chains of decisions and of transfer resources. It is not unusual for funds to be agreed by the Treasury in a donor country, passed to a development ministry and at this point an agreement is made by the development ministry to achieve certain goals with its funds which will, by necessity, be couched in general terms. The introduction of the Millennium Development Goals (MDGs) has made it easier for aid ministries to adopt these as their overall goals as they are simple and have international recognition and agreement.

Funds, then, are often passed to middle men: these can be Northern NGOs, Southern NGOs, Southern governments, commercial contractors, each with some form of agreement with the donor. Then a proportion of the resources will be passed on again by the middle men possibly to subcontractors who could be local companies, Southern NGOs, local government authorities and so forth. In some cases funds may still pass hands again to community groups, a sub-sub-contractor, a local authority, a local school. Again complexity and the level of proxy in the chain is impressive, but not always efficient nor does it make it easy to judge effectiveness. If most people are merely transferring resources at what point can we judge effectiveness and impact? Presumably this is at the point of the end-user of the funds or activity. But many of these stakeholders do not have access to or contact with the end-user so the best they can do is to ensure that the organisation they passed the funds to has done with these funds what was agreed (efficiently and honestly). Thus we can see how the main chain of feedback is around accountability.

So who has the responsibility for learning and for assessing impact? Who has the capacity to engage in learning and at what level? One problem which is often not clarified is the level at which we are pitching our learning. If I am the personnel officer in a large programme I need to know that my HR systems are adequate, that I am hiring the right people, that they are paid the right amount and so forth. There is thus a lot we can learn from any transaction which may have only a marginal relevance to whether our joint activities have met our overall goal – of reducing poverty, improving maternal health or whatever. Such organisational learning is important in itself and any improvement in the organisation will hopefully improve our ability to meet our mission.

However, we have a second problem which is linked to the nature of the aid chain. Naturally enough, different stakeholders in the various agencies in the chain will have very different needs or interests in the whole endeavour. Thus we will not all be trying to learn about the same thing. As a community leader what I want to know will be (or should be) very different from what the director of the back donor needs to know (as opposed to would like to know.[67]) So what dominates in the information chain, inevitably, is the needs of the person or organisation at the top. That this demand for a certain type of information exists would not matter if it was placed in the context of other needs. Instead, what we observe is an information system pulling towards the top, in the absence of any systems to

---

67. This difference between needing to know in order to improve ones own decision making and performance is very different from wanting to know something because of personal interest Unfortunately these are often so confused, hence the demands for too much information to pass through the chain to meet individual interests. After all, it is far more interesting to receive reports on the local political situation on somewhere where we have worked than just the dry report of activities. The end result is information overload and the collection of information for reasons no one can recall, but which may well simply reflect the personal whim of a long-departed desk officer.

serve those in other parts of the chain. Thus as we come back down the chain the power to learn from the information collected is weaker, the information is not collected and the need to give good news up the chain hinders our learning from mistakes. Those who most need to learn whether their work is having an impact are the last to have a voice in how and where the information is collected and what the questions being asked are by the M&E system. Should we therefore be surprised that after many years of trying we still find that we have a struggle between accountability and learning and that within both there is a continuous pull towards the top of the aid chain?

Addressing the Problem by Separating Accountability from Learning

One proposal which has emerged from the workshops is that we make an effort to separate accountability from learning. This has been suggested on the basis that they require completely different methodologies, audiences and approaches. It is also based on a strong feeling that although in an ideal world the two would go hand-in-hand, the reality is that we fail time after time to achieve this successful marriage. Therefore the suggestion is the 'amicable divorce' between the two, an approach where the demands of accountability and learning are seen as separate.

Accountability focuses on four main areas:

- use of resources – resources in the budget are purchased etc.,
- timing of activities – timing of activities occurs as per plan
- outputs achieved – wells drilled, schools built etc
- immediate outcomes – water provided, courses completed etc.

To achieve this requires the use of 'accounting techniques' and questions such as do we know where our resources went or can we literally say where the money went? It also needs a simple monitoring system to enable us to say whether we have indeed spent the resources as planned (activities, assets, services etc).

Learning is, then, focused on the level of more qualitative aspects of development such as the longer-term changes and impact of a programme. Although there will also be some more day-to-day learning about the process of our intervention, for example as noted above 'were our systems

up to employing people on time?', 'was our chain of decision making clear?', to be honest many of these things – although important organisationally – are of less interest to either our donors or to our end users. The latter will be particularly interested in learning whether the micro-credit has brought wealth, the clinic has reduced malaria or newly elected women councillors have acquired influence. In other words, the outcome and impact level findings are what they will be looking for. Whilst donors should also be interested in this level they are often unfortunately permanently derailed by the accountability issue. If a donor is not interested in the final impact how can they ever make a decision on future funding, both in terms of who to fund and what type of investment reaps the best developmental rewards?

The advantages of this approach are that separating accountability from learning eases demands on front line staff. Potentially a simple M&E system with a clear accountability purpose can be developed and put into practice with limited training and support. For larger organisations, including donors, it would be possible to 'contract out' the accountability to accountancy firms and retain the learning function as way of trying to improve the impact of what they do or support.

Once the issue of accountability is resolved people should be able to relax and try to be more honest and share what really has, or has not, constrained or promoted what they are trying to achieve. It also means that it would be possible to isolate certain aspects of a programme for greater attention where a particular issue arises or where a success or failure would justify greater attention.

However, the potential limitations are that the separation of accountability from learning would mean that learning could become just an optional extra, squeezed out due to time and budget considerations. With the current focus on efficiency over effectiveness this is a real danger!

In conclusion, we are faced with several challenges, but in many ways they come down to a single debate over the nature of what we think we are trying to monitor and evaluate in terms of our approach to development. It is not surprising that debates in M&E should reflect wider debates about what constitutes development and the best ways to achieve different developmental views. In our wide ranging set of workshops these differences became clear and the tensions between practitioners became perhaps more marked. Some people find that they are satisfied with an approach which equates efficiency with doing a better job, because they are confident that their underlying approach to development is right, probably does not need to be questioned and therefore merely needs to be managed well. Whilst others will not feel happy with this approach and will continue to argue for more attention both on the underlying causes of poverty and inequality as well as improved analysis of what actually makes a difference, and what impacts can and should we expect from different forms of development policy and practice. It will be important to get beyond the short-term activities to review what are the real socio-economic changes being achieved by different forms of developmental assistance and investments by civil society and the state.

We started this book by revising briefly the history of attempts to evaluate social development as reflected in main through the earlier five international conferences. The challenge now in front of us is that many of the benchmarks of good practice established over the past fifteen or more years have now either been forgotten or are being rejected or sidelined. In our regional workshops it became clear that many grass-roots development workers still find that they do need to engage with issues such as client-based M&E and how best to assess impact. However, a strong counter trend is to deny the validity of social development as a concept in favour of a very simplistic (and previously discredited) version of development as economic growth and administrative efficiency. That there is little evidence to sustain this view seems inconvenient to those propagating it, but such an outlook chimes conveniently with desires of public bodies to disengage from the time-consuming, complex and messy aspects of development. Therefore, it serves them to resort to a simple cheap form of delivery. Those directly engaging in development often find that however much they would like to a retreat to a simpler view of development that is not a luxury they can afford.

If we are even halfway correct in our analysis of the global push towards a new state-dominated and economic view of development, and our identification of a desire for administratively simple forms of delivery mechanism which lend themselves to organisationally neat forms of M&E, then the conclusion is clear: we must loudly and clearly re-state the case not only for key concepts such as participatory M&E, but also for the very concept of social development itself.

Facilitators' Notes

HOME GROUP

All participants will be asked to join a Home Group for the duration of the workshop. These home groups are designed to help participants evaluate the conference during the process. They are reasonably small groups which should enable all delegates to discuss the day and assist the facilitators to ensure they are providing a well facilitated conference where participantsí needs are met. There will be twelve home groups of ten people each these will be randomly selected and names allocated.

During the day, Home Group members should check with each other that there are no language or other practical problems. If there are, these should be raised with the facilitators.

At the end of each day, all Home Groups should meet together for about 15 minutes to discuss the following:

- What went well today?
- What could have been better?
- Suggestions for the remainder of the conference.

Each group should select one workshop member to represent the group's views to the facilitators at the End-of-Day Review Meetings.

INTRAC facilitators will hold end of day review meetings to hear what the participants have fed back and adjust the programme if necessary for the following day.

+	-
People are able to speak in small groups	Time-consuming at the end of the day
Assists with internalising what has happened that day Quick feedback from participants	Everyone in the homegroup needs to participate
Allows facilitators to hear 'democratic' feedback	
Programme can be adjusted in 'real time' and problems pre-empted	

CAFÉ TABLES

The Themed Café tables are designed to allow groups of up to eight participants to meet in the evening to discuss a theme that they are particularly interested in and record their discussion. Coffee or wine can be brought to the 'café'.

Each table will be allocated a theme. A poster listing each theme will be on display during the day so people can select their topic in advance. Two tables will have blank themes so new ideas can be added at the time.

The discussions will be free-thinking and participants will be asked to jot down any notes they feel would be good to share on the paper tablecloths. These will then be put on the walls of the conference centre on Tuesday for all to see.

Facilitator / Rapporteur Notes

INTRAC facilitators will be needed to help ensure there are ten tables placed in one room with eight chairs per table. Paper tablecloths will be provided and the facilitators will be expected to collect them and display them appropriately.

+	-
Networking	Needs better facilitation
Documenting an informal, free-flowing exchange	Comments not always pertinent to the topic
Self-selected topics	Could have had better feedback and follow-up
Self-selected groups	Someone needs to be doodling to make sure discussion is actually captured

Key Recommendations:
CASCADING EXERCISE

Participants will be asked to contribute to this dynamic participatory methodology to produce KEY RECOMMENDATIONS FOR THE FUTURE! This exercise wraps up the last day.

All participants are expected to negotiate for their suggestions to be put forward as key recommendations of the workshop.

Stage 1: Pairs

Participants will work in pairs. Each pair will be asked to discuss and agree on **3 key recommendations** that have emerged from the conference and they feel are important to take forward. These will be recorded on coloured cards (one recommendation per card).

Stage 2: Groups of 4

Each pair will be asked to join another pair and between them they will be asked to negotiate which **3 key recommendations**, out of the previous two pairs' six recommendations, are the most important to the group. From each group of four there will hence be three key recommendations, with three discarded. These will be recorded on coloured cards (one recommendation per card).

The key recommendations that are not used will be kept by the facilitators and included in the final outcomes of the workshop.

Stage 3: Groups of 8

Each group of four will be asked to join another group of four and between the eight participants they will be asked to negotiate the **3 key recommendations** again. These will be recorded on coloured cards (one recommendation per card).

The key recommendations not used will be kept by the facilitators and included in the final outputs of the workshop.

Stage 4: Groups of 16

By the time the group size reaches 16, participants simply rank their six remaining insights in order of preference. This is done by voting – each participant gets two or three stickers ('votes') which they stick on their favoured recommendations (or all three on one). This makes it easy to see which recommendations have the most support.

The key recommendations not used will be kept by the facilitators and included in the final outputs of the workshop.

Stage 5: Groups of 32

Groups of 32 could be used, but at the Sixth Evaluation Conference that was considered too large. At this stage, the recommendation cards were collected, overlaps or similar ideas were noted, and the cards were ranked in order of most votes.

The key recommendations not used will be kept by the facilitators and included in the final outputs of the workshop.

Summary

The facilitators will expect to receive a maximum of **12 key recommendations** from the workshop which will be presented at the key recommendations summary.

Facilitator / Rapporteur Notes

The INTRAC facilitators' responsibilities will be to ensure everyone is in a group throughout the exercise. As we will not be certain of the number of participants until Friday morning we will decide on the groupings then.

It is important that *ALL* the facilitators are available throughout the sessions as there may be a need to broker any disputes between the groups when they try to bring six key recommendations down to three. It is also essential that all discarded cards are collected.

Each step of the process will provide different coloured cards.

+	-
A way to synthesise findings from a large group	Some participants feel marginalised and not listened to
Negotiation skills strengthening makes people focus	May eliminate creativity – consensus on 'grey mush' recommendations
Each idea needs to be thoroughly justified – no space for lazy thinking	
Quickly realise what is NOT important	
One charismatic person's 'pet idea' can't get far	

MARKET PLACE

Participants are invited to set up 'market stalls' to display examples of their M&E experiences, for instance, success stories or lessons learnt during projects. This is an ideal opportunity for participants to share their M&E work with each other.

Materials displayed can include posters, pictures, publications and leaflets. INTRAC will provide tables, flip charts and other materials.

Set up: Materials are to be set up early. INTRAC Staff will assist and allocate an appropriate space for materials.

On the Monday participants will be invited to explore the market place and begin to get a feel for the type of work other participants are involved in.

Posters on the regional M&E workshops that were held in preparation for the conference will also be on display.

Facilitator / Rapporteur Notes

The INTRAC facilitators will assist with setting up the stalls on Sunday and Monday.

Materials will be placed in one or two rooms (to be selected by facilitators on Saturday in advance).

+	-
Networking	Noisy
Learning	Need to provide plenty of time
Sharing	Needs space
Makes participants prepare in advance	Favours organisations with nice visual materials

Exchange of Methodologies: Speed Exchange

Participants are asked to sit on chairs in two circles – one inside the other, chairs facing each other, so that each person sits facing another person.

Participants pair up and spend three minutes exchanging methodologies. A bell will sound and participants move on to new people at three-minute intervals. Only the people in the outer circle move – each one e.g. one chair to their right (we moved three chairs because you might have already heard the person sitting one chair away), and talk to the new person sitting opposite.

This is essentially an 'express' networking exercise, which also pairs participants who would not necessarily interact during breaks.

Before the session prepare a short list of your methodology experiences and a few questions to ask other participants. The trick is to get as much information about a person as possible in those precious few minutes. Go straight for the facts.

Business cards and a notebook will also come in handy.

+	-
Good individual input	Noisy
Excellent for networking	120 participants was a bit too much
Links people who would not necessarily talk otherwise	Needs to be held at the most appropriate time in the conference
At the Conference, participants found they learned about unexpected aspects of each others' work and made interesting connections.	Cumbersome to set up
	'Speed dating' stigma

THEMATIC WORKING GROUPS

Five thematic groups will be run simultaneously. Participants will be asked to sign up for the groups in advance. Those that sign up early will be more likely to get their first choice. Each participant will be able to attend two thematic groups, one on Day 1 and another on Day 2.

Speakers' papers and abstracts are available online at:

http://www.intrac.org/pages/themepapers.html

Each group will be asked to choose a chair and a scribe who will prepare a flip chart for a gallery walk, to be displayed. INTRAC will provide a rapporteur for each session.

For the Tuesday Gallery Session one member from each group will stand next to the poster to answer questions from other participants.

Facilitator / Rapporteur Notes

The INTRAC facilitators' responsibilities will be to ensure everyone has signed up for a group on each of the two days. They also need to ensure that there is a reasonably even spread of delegates across the groups.

For each thematic working group the same INTRAC rapporteur needs to be present at both sessions, i.e. on day one and day two. This is to ensure the note taking from the two groups will be easier to pull together for dissemination by the facilitators' team on day three.

+	-
Working in smaller groups	Reporting back is time-consuming
Focuses the discussion	Not all the themes are covered
Better outputs	

Geographic Working Groups

Six geographic groups will be run simultaneously. Participants will be part of the group that fits their geographic region. These groups will look at the thematic issues and will consider which issues are a priority in their region. The aim at the Conference is to articulate functioning methods, what does not work, and what could be done differently.

Each group will be asked to choose a chair and a scribe who will prepare a flip chart as feedback at the end of the session. One member from each group will stand next to the poster to answer questions from other participants. INTRAC will provide a rapporteur for each session.

+	-
Working in smaller groups	Reporting back is time-consuming
Focuses the discussion	Not all the themes are covered
Better outputs	
Opportunity to build on regional M&E workshops	
Geographical grouping means discussions are more likely to touch on relevant day-to-day concerns.	

List of Participants at Sixth Evaluation Conference

Louis Acheampong, **Social Support Foundation**
Jerry Adams, **INTRAC**
Katharine Al Ju'beh, **Sight Savers International**
Muhtari Aminu-Kano, **BirdLife International**
Vera Alpar, **St.Istvan University/ Ministry of Youth, Family and Social Affairs and Equal Opportunities**
Marlen Arkesteijn, **Capturing Development: M&E through video**
Dwi Astuti, **Bina Desa**
Dhan Bahadur Nepali, **Oppressed Society Deliverance Organization**
Oliver Bakewell, **International Migration Institute, Oxford**
Rema Nair Balasundaram, **Independent Consultant**
Kaustuv Kanti Bandyopadhyay, **PRIA**
Marie Barck, **Sida**
Gert Bekebrede, **Prisma**
Karin van den Belt, **NiZA**
Monica Billgren, **Forum Syd**
Monica Blagescu, **One World Trust**
Neeltje Blommestein, **IICD**
Barbara Brubacher, **Interkerkelijk Vredesberaad**
Mattias Brunander, **Diakonia**
Jennifer Chapman, **Independent Consultant**
Youding Chen, **China NPO Network**

Taurai Chigunwe, **Civic Education Network Trust**
Francisco de Assis Comarú, **Polis Institute**
Julius Court, **Overseas Development Institute**
Fortunat Diener, **Community Action Program Iraq**
Olga Djanaeva, **Rural Women's NGO 'Alga'**
Nomvula Dlamini, **Community Development Resource Association**
Deepak Dorje Tamang, **Search-Nepal**
Aroma Dutta, **PRIP Trust**
Anju Dwivedi, **PRIA**
Nikolay M Elizarov, **Amnesty International**
Ivar Evensmo, **NORAD**
Mohammad Fareed Waqfi, **Coordination for Humanitarian Assistance**
Silva Ferretti, **ActionAid International**
Mary Finn, **Concern Worldwide**
Joanna Fisher, **Christian Aid**
Innesa Frantz, **Institute for Development Cooperation, Almaty**
Nacho Wilhelmi Garcia, **DARA International**
Beniam Gebrezghi, **Sida**
Shanti George, **Bernard van Leer Foundation**
Alaa Mahmoud Ghalayini, **Welfare Association Consortium**
Hugh Goyder, **INTRAC Associate**
Gerhild Gurtler, **DW/ Bread for the World**
Ben Haagsma, **I/C Consult**
Ehtisham ul Hasan, **Save the Children**
Henrik Herber, **Americas Swedish Red Cross**
Silvia Hidalgo, **DARA International**
Catherine Hine, **Oxfam**
Charlotte Imbert, **BOND**
Rudoph Jansen, **Lawyers for Human Rights**
Helene Jeansson, **Forum Syd**
Adan Wario Kabelo, **MS Kenya**
Abdelrahim Kamel Moustafa Alasa'd, **Welfare Association Consortium**
Muthialganesan Karrunanithi, **All Women and Rural Development Trust**
Willi Kawohl, **DW/Bread for the World**
Niels Keijzer, **European Centre for Development Policy Management**
Samia Liaquat Ali Khan, **Minority Rights Group International**
Yogesh Kumar, **Samarthan**

Torunn Kvamme, **Norwegian Red Cross**
Li Lifan, **Center for Central Asia Studies**
Linda Lönnqvist, **INTRAC**
Odenda Lumumba, **Kenya Land Alliance**
Michela Lupi, **Trócaire**
Kennedy Lweya, **IMA International**
Osei Lydia, **Foundation for Environmental Development, Improvement and Protection**
Don Marquez, **ANGOC**
Sarah McCan, **Trócaire**
Anne-Marie McCarthy, **Irish Missionary Resource Service**
Esther Mebrahtu, **INTRAC Associate**
Marta Marañón Medina, **DARA International**
Roger Miranda, **Independent Consultant**
Noel Molony, **Trócaire East Africa**
Agustin Moya, **DARA International**
Caroline Mukosa, **MS Zambia**
Ane Mygland, **NDN**
Joseph Narh, **Hopelink International**
Kebba Ngumbo Sima, ActionAid International
Marie Jose Niesten, **MDF**
Caterina Occhio, **Nehem International**
Sarah Okwaare, **Actionaid International Uganda**
Teobaldo Pinzas, **ETC Andes**
Anne-Marijke Podt, **IICD**
Brian Pratt, **INTRAC**
Padma Ratnayake, **South Asia Partnership Sri Lanka**
Pia Reierson, **Adra Norway**
Wouter Rijneveld, **Woord en Daad**
Mara Rodriguez, **VSO**
Gabriela Romo, **INTRAC**
Tessa Roorda, **PSO**
Jo Rowlands, **Oxfam**
Doreen Ruta, **MS Uganda**
Rens Rutten, **CORDAID**
Aliya Salahuddin, **International Media Corporation**
Sadiqa Salahuddin, **Indus Resource Centre**

Helen Schneider, **VSO**
Johannes R Schot, **CAFOD**
Mohd Shafiq Yari, **Rural Rehabilitation Association for Afghanistan**
Peter Sigsgaard, **MS Denmark**
Reinhard Skinner, **Bernard van Leer Foundation**
Luis Soberon, **Pontificia Universidad Católica del Perú**
Rajan Soni, **International Organisation Development Ltd**
Susan Stewart, **University of Mannheim**
Elke Stumpf, **Working Group on Development and Peace, GTZ**
Johan Svensson, **Life and Peace Institute**
Marcella Tam, **PSO**
Marleen ter Haar Romeny, **Right To Play Netherlands**
Alix Tiernan, **Trócaire**
Virginia Tortella, **DARA International**
Janet Townsend, **University of Newcastle upon Tyne**
Martine Van de Velde, **Consultant**
Joel Van der Hart **Compassion International**
Enrique Vasquez, **Universidad del Pacifico**
Elizabeth Wade-Brown, **CAFOD**
Vivien Walden, **Oxfam**
Patricia Wall, **Development Studies Centre**
Zhongping Wang, China NPO Network
Chris Wardle, INTRAC Associate
Elizabeth Webber, VSO
Senorina Wendoh, Transform Africa
Zoë Wilkinson, INTRAC
Robyn Willford, **Concern Worldwide**
Mike Williams, **Trócaire**
Rebecca Wrigley, **INTRAC**
Katie Wright-Revolledo, **INTRAC**
Padmavathi Yedla, **Save The Children**
Sjoerd Zanen, **MDF**
Lada Zimina, **Skillshare International**
Melia Zulu, **Episcopal Conference of Malawi**
Dirk Johannes Zuurmond, **Plan**

Bibliography

ActionAid (2005) *Real Aid: An Agenda for Making Aid Work.*
www.actionaid.org.uk/wps/content/documents/real_aid.pdf

Adams, J (2005), *A Paper Looking at the Role of the Media in Humanitarian Disasters and Questioning whether they have a Role in Monitoring and Evaluation*INTRAC.

Adong, R. (2005) 'Comments on the Scoping Paper', document prepared for the *Southern Voices Project*
www.odi.org.uk/ffa/workshop_nov05/Comments-Scoping%20paper/
RosemaryAdong.pdf

AFRODAD (2003) *Reality Check on Development Aid: Toward A More Responsive Aid Regime In The Context of AU and NEPAD*

AFRODAD (2003) Trade and Debt Blockages-Which Way Forward? Financing for Development and Debt, Harare, Zimbabwe.

Alikan F, Kyei P, Mawdsley E, Porter G, Raju S, Townsend J, Varma R. (2007) *NGOs and the State in the Twenty-first Century*INTRAC.
www.intrac.org/resources_database.php?id=282

Bakewell, O. et al. (2003) *Sharpening the Development Process,* INTRAC.

Bakewell, O. (2006) 'Complexity and Simplicity: Addressing Accountability and Learning', *SIDA's Logical Framework Review.*

Bakewell, O. and Garbutt, A. (2006) *The use and abuse of the logical framework approach,* Sida
www.sida.se/shared/jsp/download.jsp?f=LFA-review.pdf&a=21025

Bhattacharya, D. (2005) 'Southern Voices on the Evolving International Aid Architecture – A Review of Literature from Selected Asian Countries', *Southern Voices Project*
www.odi.org.uk/ffa/southern_documents.html.

Booth, D. (2005) 'Aid to Africa: More Doesn't Have to Mean Worse', *ODI Opinions*. Overseas Development Institute.
www.odi.org.uk/publications/opinions/43_aid_to_africa_june05.pdf

Campodónico, H. and Valderrama, M. (2005b) 'Some Comments on Alina Rocha's and Andrew Rogerson's Scoping Paper "Which Way the Future of Aid?"', *Southern Voices Project,*
www.odi.org.uk/ffa/workshop_nov05/Comments-scoping%20paper/
campodonico-Valderrama.pdf

Chirwa, W. & Nyirenda, M. (2002) *People's Participation in Policymaking: The Case of Malawi's PRSP: A Research Report for Christian Aid*

Dávila, C. (2005) 'Comments Prepared for the Southern Voices Project', *Southern Voices Project,*
www.odi.org.uk/ffa/southern_documents.html

De Renzio, P. (2005) *Scaling Up Versus Absorptive Capacity: Challenges and Opportunities for Reaching the MDGs in Africa* ODI Briefing Paper www.odi.org.uk/publications/briefing/bp_may05_absorptive_capacity.pdf

Dlamini, N. (2006) *Linking M&E to Organisational Learning*, CDRA, South Africa

Dwivendi, A. *Citizen Monitoring*, PRIA, India

Earle, L (ed.) (2004) *Creativity and Constraint: Grassroots Monitoring and Evaluation and the International Aid Arena*, INTRAC.

Earle, L. et al (2005) *The Development of Civil Society in Central Asia* INTRAC.

Easterly, W. (2006) *The White Man's Burden* Oxford, Oxford University Press.

Fernando, P. (2005a) 'Southern Voices on the Evolving International Aid Architecture: Commentary on a Review of the Literature from Selected Asian Countries by Debapriya Bhattacharya', *Southern Voices Project* www.odi.org.uk/ffa/southern_documents.html

Fernando, P. (2005b) 'Comments on the ODI Scoping Paper: Which way the future of aid? Southern Civil Society perspectives on current debates on reform to the international aid system', *Southern Voices Project* www.odi.org.uk/ffa/workshop_nov05/Comments-Scoping%20paper/ PriyanthiFernandodoc.pdf

Gariyo, Z. (2002) *The PRSP Process in Uganda* Discussion Paper No. 5 Uganda Debt Network, www.udn.or.ug/pub/prsp.pdf

Goyder, H. (2006) *What Stops Us Learning? Some Reflections from recent Humanitarian Evaluations*, Paper Presented at Sixth Evaluation Conference.

INTRAC (2007) *Civil Society Perspectives Strengthening the Poverty Impact of the Paris Declaration: through Gender Equality, Human Rights and Social Exclusion:Phase One: Literature Review* www.dfid.gov.uk/procurement/files/civil-society.pdf

Isooba, M. (2005) 'Southern Voices for Change in the International Aid Architecture: Listening and Learning from the Voices of the Civil Society. What Kind of Difference?', *Southern Voices Project* www.odi.org.uk/ffa/southern_documents.html

James, R. & Malunga, C. (2006) *The Rise and Pitfalls of Civil Society Networks in Malawi*, INTRAC www.intrac.org/docs/CSO%20Networks%202006%20_final%20June%205%20 2006_.pdf

Koergaard, O. (ed.) (2001) *Learning for Democratic Citizenship*, Association for World Education and the Danish University of Education.

Kumar, Y. (2006) *Monitoring and Evaluation of Advocacy Campaigns: Opportunities and Challenges*, Samarthan – Centre for Development Support. www.intrac.org/docs.php/2301/TWG%202%20Advocacy%20%20Paper%20 Yogesh%20Kumar.doc

Lifuka, R. (2005) 'Draft Issues Review Report', *Southern Voices Project* www.odi.org.uk/ffa/southern_documents.html

Marquez, N. and Debuque, T. *Ensuring Household Food Security* ANGOC, Philippines

Marsden, D. & Oakley, P. (1990) *Evaluating Social Development*, Oxfam.

Marsden, D. Oakley, P. & Pratt, B. (1994) *Measuring the Process: Guidelines for Evaluating Social Development*, INTRAC.

Maxwell, S. (2005) *The Washington Consensus is Dead! Long Live the Meta-narrative!*, ODI Working Paper No. 243, Overseas Development Institute, http://www.odi.org.uk/publications/working_papers/wp243.pdf

Mebrahtu, E. (2003) *Putting Policy into Practice: INGO Experiences in Ethiopia*, INTRAC

Mohanty, R. (2001) *Village level Institution as Forum for Community Participation in Development Experiences from Watershed, Forest and drinking Water Management Project in Uttaranchal.*

Moldesheva, A. & Buxton, C, (2006) *NGOs in Central Asia: Partners in East-West Dialogue*, Paper presented at the ISS Conference, Netherlands. http://dprn.fss.uu.nl/No%2025%20Non-EU%20Europe,%20Caucacus,%20 Central%20Asia.pdf

Mwakasege, C. (2005c) 'A Review on Southern Voices for Change in International Aid Architecture – the Uganda Experience'. *Southern Voices Project.* www.odi.org.uk/ffa/southern_documents.html

Oakley, P. et al, (1991) *Projects with People:The Practice of Participation in Rural Development*, International Labour Organisation.

Oakley, P, Pratt, B. & Clayton A. (eds) (1998) *Outcomes and Impact: Evaluating Change in Social Development*, INTRAC.

Oakley, P. & Clayton, A. (2000) *The Monitoring and Evaluation of Empowerment* INTRAC www.intrac.org/docs/OPS26final.pdf

Oakley, P (ed.) (2001) *Evaluating Empowerment: Reviewing the Concept and Practice* INTRAC.

OECD-DAC (2002) *A Development Co-operation Lens on Terism Prevention: Key Entry Points for Action*, DAC Guidelines and Reference Series. www.oecd.org/dataoecd/17/4/16085708.pdf

Pankanji, A. (2002) 'Experience and lessons of Strengthening Citizen's Monitoring in Jharkhand: A Citizenship Perspective', *Innovation in Civil Society*, Volume 1, No. 2.

Pratt B. (2005) *Paris Agenda: Aid Harmonisation Efficiency versus Effectiveness.* Paper Presented at Netherlands Conference, INTRAC.

Prasad K.V. and Prasad, A. (2005) *Understanding and Strengthening NGO Networks* PRIA www.intrac.org/docs.php/2105/Understanding%20and%20Strengthening%20 NGO%20Networks.pdf

Reality of Aid (2004) *An Independent Review of Poverty Reduction and Development Assistance: Focus on Governance and Human Rights* ed Books.

Riddell, R. (1997) *Searching for Impact and Methods: NGO Preparation Synthesis* Report Prepared for OECD-DAC Expert Group on Evaluation. Blue Series: Finland.

Rogerson, A. (2005a) *Giving, Forgiving and Taking Back: Why Continue to Make Soft Loans to Very Poor Countries* www.odi.org.uk/publications/opinions

Rogerson, A. (2005b) 'Aid Harmonisation and Alignment: Bridging the Gaps between Reality and the Paris Reform Agenda', *Development Policy Review* 23 (5):531–52.

Salahuddin, S. (2006) *Introduction to Issues That We are Grappling With* Indus Resource Centre, Pakistan

Salahuddin, A. (2005) *Assessing the Role of the Media in Humanitarian Disasters* International Media Corporation, Pakistan

Smillie, S. (1995) *The Alms Bazaar: Altruism Under Fire – Non Profit Organisations and International Development*, IDRC/ITDG Publishing.

Soni, R. (2006) *Results-based Country Programme Evaluation*, PARC India.

Starky, P. (1997) *Networking for Development*, IFRTD

Surr, M. (1995) *Evaluations of Non-Government Organisations (NGOs) Development Projects: Synthesis Report*, Overseas Development Administration

Tandon, R. (2002) *Linking Citizenship, Participation and Accountability: A Perspective from PRIA*, IDS Bulletin Volume 33 No 20.

Tendler, J. (1993a) *New Lessons from Old Projects: The Workings of Rural Development in Northeast Brazil. A World. Bank Operations Evaluation Study* www.un.org/esa/socdev/poverty/papers/tendler2.pdf

Tujan, A. (2005a) 'Comments on the Draft Scoping Paper: The Politics of Aid', *Southern Voices Project* www.odi.org.uk/ffa/workshop_nov05/ Comments-Scoping%20paper/ ATujan.pdf.

Tujan, A. (2005b) 'Comments on the Review of Literature – Asia', *Southern Voices Project*, www.odi.org.uk/ffa/southern_documents.html

Van der Blcek, (1999) *Guidelines to Participatory Innovation Development*

Van de Walle, N. (2005) *Overcoming Stagnation in Aid-Dependent Countries*. *Washington*, DC: Center for Global Development.

Wallace, T. & Chapman, J. (2005) 'An investigation into the reality behind NGO rhetoric of downward accountability' in Earle, L. (ed.), *Creativity and Constraint: Grassroots Monitoring and Evaluation and the International Aid Arena*

Index

www.ingramcontent.com/pod-product-compliance
Lightning Source LLC
Chambersburg PA
CBHW070933030426
42336CB00014BA/2655